Medical Science

THE STUDY OF SCIENCE

Medical Science

Edited by Maya Bayden

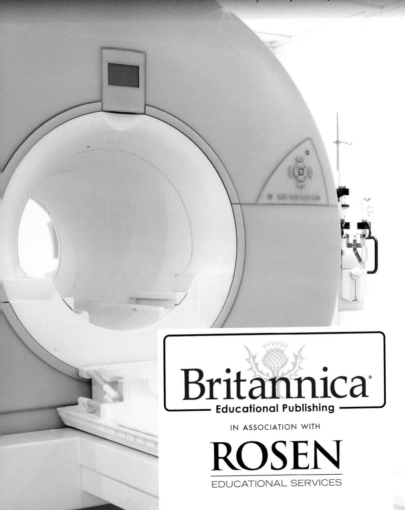

Britannica®
Educational Publishing

IN ASSOCIATION WITH

ROSEN
EDUCATIONAL SERVICES

Published in 2017 by Britannica Educational Publishing (a trademark of Encyclopædia Britannica, Inc.) in association with The Rosen Publishing Group, Inc.
29 East 21st Street, New York, NY 10010

Distributed exclusively by Rosen Publishing.
To see additional Britannica Educational Publishing titles, go to rosenpublishing.com.

First Edition

Britannica Educational Publishing
J.E. Luebering: Director, Core Reference Group
Anthony L. Green: Editor, Compton's by Britannica

Rosen Publishing
Maya Bayden: Editor
Nelson Sá: Art Director
Brian Garvey: Designer
Cindy Reiman: Photography Manager
Karen Huang: Photo Research
Introduction and conclusion by Kara Rogers.

Library of Congress Cataloging-in-Publication Data

Medical science / edited by Maya Bayden.
    pages cm.— (The study of science)
Audience: Grades 7–12.
Includes bibliographical references and index.
ISBN 978-1-68048-229-4 (library bound : alk. paper)
1. Medicine—Juvenile literature. I. Bayden, Maya, editor.
R130.5.M418 2016
610 — dc23

                                                    2015018808

Manufactured in China

Photo credits: Cover, p. 3 sfam photo/Shutterstock.com; p. 10 Science & Society Picture Library/Getty Images; pp. 15, 18 © Photos.com/Thinkstock; p. 21 Heritage Images/Hulton Archive/Getty Images; pp. 25, 38, 44 National Library of Medicine, Bethesda, Maryland; p. 31 Omikron/Science Source/Getty Images; p. 42 Encyclopaedia Britannica, Inc.; p. 51 © Corbis; p. 55 Jetta Productions/The Image Bank/Getty Images; pp. 68, 106 BSIP/Universal Images Group/Getty Images; p. 70 Michael Blann/Digital Vision/Thinkstock; p. 74 Darren Baker/Shutterstock.com; p. 78 Thomas Barwick/Taxi/Getty Images; p. 81 Peter Parks/AFP/Getty Images; p. 84 Janice Haney Carr/CDC; pp. 86, 113 © AP Images; p. 91 De Agostini Picture Library/Getty Images; p. 94 Courtesy of the National Museum of Health and Medicine, Armed Forces Institute of Pathology, Washington, D.C.; p. 100 Digital Vision/Thinkstock; p. 102 Tino Soriano/National Geographic Image Collection/Getty Images; p. 108 Robson Fernandjes/picture-alliance/dpa/AP Images; p. 111 © J. Fujishima/B.W. Halstead, World Life Research Institute; p. 115 Centers for Disease Control and Prevention (CDC) (Image Number: 6372); p. 117 Terry Vine/The Image Bank/Getty Images; p. 119 Science Source; p. 122 ullstein bild/Getty Images; cover and interior pages backgrounds and borders © iStockphoto.com/LuMaxArt.

CONTENTS

CONTENTS

INTRODUCTION

The practice of medicine—the science and art of preventing, alleviating, and curing disease—is an ancient profession. Healers with varying degrees of knowledge and skills have long sought to restore the health or relieve the distress of the sick and injured. Historically, that often meant doing little more than offering sympathy to the patient while nature took its course. Today, however, practitioners of medicine have several millennia of medical advances on which to base the care of their patients. The vast majority of those advances are the product of scientific discovery.

As with astronomy and physics, the application of science, through the systematic study of nature and the accurate recording of natural fact, revolutionized medicine. The uptake of science, however, initially was very slow in medicine. Indeed, the first to place disease in the realm of natural rather than supernatural causes was the ancient Greek physician Hippocrates, who lived in the 5th and 4th centuries BCE. His writings, which make up the Hippocratic Collection, greatly influenced Greek philosophers and physicians. However, literate and educated individuals who could apply this knowledge were few in number. As a result, the practice of medicine remained largely based on precedent, with treatments rooted in folklore and magic.

In fact, it was not until the 16th and 17th centuries, during the Renaissance and the Enlightenment that followed, that Western medicine became firmly grounded in science. Anatomical and physiological revelations were many during those periods, owing to the detailed work of physicians such as Andreas Vesalius, who corrected historical errors in descriptions of human anatomy, and William Harvey, who provided the first complete description of the circulation of blood through the human body.

Advances in surgery and in the understanding of disease processes ensued, and tools to aid in disease prevention, diagnosis, and treatment were discovered and developed. Paramount among those advances was vaccination, demonstrated convincingly at the end of the 18th century by English surgeon Edward Jenner, who successfully inoculated a young boy against smallpox. Early the following century, French physician René Laënnec invented the stethoscope for listening to sounds produced within the body.

CHARTA PARVAS ALIQVOT FIGVRAS COM

PLECTENS, QVAE FIGVRAE AD COMMONSTRANDAM VE
narum arteriarum̄q̄ simul commissarum seriem paratæ, ac in pagina m 3, aut numero 313 insignita obuiæ,
ueniunt agglutinandæ.

PRIMA.   TERTIA.   SEXTA.

VT figuras hac
charta inpreß as commo
de suis sedibus glutines,
illæq̄ ualidiores reddan
tur, primùm præsenti
chartæ membranam sub
glutinabis, singulasq̄ fi
guras à superflua papy
ro resecabis. PRI
MA, quæ uenæ pa
ri carentis distributio-
nem proponit. magnæ figu-
gure tergo illic uenit cō
mittenda, ubi caua cau-
dex eam uenam promit.
ac o in utrisque figuris
scriptū spectatur. SE
CVNDA, ubi à
redundanti papyro cir-
cuncisa erit, duas partes
constituet, quarum supe-
rior uenam arteriam que
dextri lateris exprimit,
sub pectoris osse superio
rem abdominis sedem pe-
tentes. Huius itaq̄ par-
tis q̄ admagnæ figuræ
q̄ figitur, ꝗ * ad ra-
mun qui ad dextrum la-
tus ꝗ o in magna
figura occurrit. Cæte-
rùm humilior pars uenæ
arteriamq̄ exprimens,
quæ inferiorem abdomi-
nis sedem implicant, illic
est iungenda, ubi earum
radices iuxta l in dex-
tro latere spectantur.
TERTIA
cæteris dignior, uenæ
porte distributionem si-
mul cū arterijs illam con-
comitantibus, magnā que
inferioris membranæ o-
menti portione et liene
pariter exprimens, ad ea
uem iecoris sedem maiori
figuræ nectetur, ubi ꝗ
ꝑ, s, et contermini ali-
quot characteres in utris
que figuris spectantur.
QVARTA
portionem gibbæ sedis ie
coris proponens, nō inu-
tiliter ueluti ex puncto il
lic glutinabitur, ubi A
inter ſ et F maioris
figuræ consistit.
QVINTA
præter testes ipsorumq̄
inuolucra, et urinarios
meatus, uenas arteriasq̄
seminales ostendens, illic
est committenda, ubi n in
ambabus figuris obuium

SECVNDA.   QVARTA.   SEPTIMA.

QVINTA.   OCTAVA

est, aut ubi uena seminalis arterie primùm iungitur, meatusq̄ urinarij illis subijciuntur.
SEXTA primùm sub SEPTIMA uenit glutinanda. Septima enim uesicæ et penis anteriorem sedem proponit, una cum ua
sis quæ uesicam et umbilico asscribimus. Sexta autem humiliorem penis superficiem in hoc expreßimus, ut tota figura ex ambabus illis consurgēs, charactere ꝑ
super quintæ figuræ ꝑ necti queat, ac postmodum penis instar S implicari.
OCTAVA figura mulieris uesicam et umbilici uasa, urinariorumq̄ meatuum portionem continens, maiori non est committenda, sed illi figuræ quæ in chartæ tergo ubi maior impreßa est, uterum ipsum, uenas et arterias seminariaq̄ uasa commonstrat. I ungetur itaq̄ octaua ad paruam
illam figuram ubi n occurrit, uenaq̄ seminalis arteriæ committitur: nexus uerò fiet urinarijs tantùm meatibus, proportione à uesicæ situ sumpta.

m 3

Also in the 19th century, some of the first pharmaceuticals were introduced, including the painkiller morphine and the anesthetics ether and chloroform. In 1865 British surgeon Joseph Lister introduced carbolic acid as a means of protecting patients from infection during surgery, opening the way to antiseptic medicine. Lister's breakthrough helped verify germ theory, which proposed that microorganisms were the cause of certain diseases.

The scientific basis of medicine continued to expand in the 20th and early 21st centuries. Of particular importance during those periods were advances in cell biology, genetics, and biomedical engineering, which greatly improved scientists' understanding of disease. With that scientific knowledge has come major progress in diagnosis and therapeutics. Vast improvements in health care, which in many places worldwide is now highly structured, have enabled physicians to more efficiently meet the medical needs of individual patients while also promoting the health of populations. As a result, the impact of mortality on populations has decreased significantly. In 2015 in the United States, an estimated 8.15 deaths occurred among every 1,000 people—a

Shown is a page of anatomical diagrams of human organs taken from Andreas Vesalius's *Seven Books on the Structure of the Human Body*, published in 1543.

vast improvement from the year 1900, when the rate was about 17.6 deaths for every 1,000 people.

In the pages that follow, readers will learn about the scientific advances that took medicine from the realm of magic to the cutting edge of technological development. Chapters on the major branches of medicine—the specialties that have come to define modern medical practice and health care—offer insight into the diagnosis, treatment, and management of disease. Special sections on epidemiology, surgery, and pharmacology explore key issues and trends, providing a unique glimpse into the ongoing progress that underlies modern medicine.

CHAPTER 1

HISTORY OF MEDICINE

E vidence of attempts to care for the sick and injured predates written records. Skulls found in Europe and South America dating as far back as 10,000 BCE have shown that the practice of trepanning, or trephining (removal of a portion of the skull bone), was not uncommon. This operation, performed by many early peoples, including Native Americans, was probably done to release evil spirits that were thought to be the source of illness. Yet, in many cases, it proved to be the medically correct thing to do—opening the skull can relieve pressure and pain caused by brain tumors and head injuries.

Indeed, much of early medicine was closely identified with pagan religions and superstitions. Illness was attributed to angry gods or evil spirits. Prayers, incantations, and other rituals were used to appease the gods or ward off demons—and thereby drive off disease. Nonetheless, the ancients did not entirely

lack valid medical knowledge. In fact, through observation and experience, they acquired considerable wisdom about sickness and its prevention and relief.

The book of Leviticus in the Hebrew Bible described quarantine regulations and sanitary practices that were used to prevent the spread of leprosy and plague. The ancient Romans realized the importance of sanitation to health and built sewers, systems that drained waste-water from public baths, and aqueducts that provided clean water.

EGYPTIAN MEDICINE

The ancient Egyptians were among the first to use certain herbs and drugs, including castor oil, senna, and opium. They also set and splinted fractured bones using techniques remarkably similar to those of modern medicine. Egyptians were reputed to be skilled diagnosticians. For instance, medical papyrus from about 1600 BCE, which is believed to be a copy of a text from about 3000 BCE, described 58 sick patients, of whom 42 were given specific diagnoses. However, though the Egyptians practiced mummification, which involved removing and dehydrating most of the internal organs of the dead, they apparently did not study those organs, as their knowledge of anatomy was quite limited.

GREEK AND ROMAN MEDICINE

Hippocrates (460–375 BCE), known as the "father of Western medicine," was an admired physician and teacher who rejected the notion that disease was punishment sent by the gods; rather, he believed it had natural causes. Hippocrates put forth a doctrine that attributed health and disease to four bodily humors, or fluids—blood, black bile, yellow bile, and phlegm. He believed that the humors were well balanced in a healthy person, but various disturbances or imbalances in them caused disease. At that time, his humoral theory seemed highly scientific. In fact, doctors diagnosed and treated illnesses based on the four humors well into the 19th century.

Hippocrates, undated bust

Knowing that he could not cure most diseases, Hippocrates tended to recommend conservative measures such as exercise, rest, and cleanliness. By contrast, for fever, which he thought was caused by an excess of blood in the body, he recommended the drastic measure of bloodletting. The practice of bloodletting, which was thought to have many therapeutic effects, was used for more than two thousand years and undoubtedly hastened the deaths of countless patients who might otherwise have recovered.

Hippocrates is best known today for his ethical code (Hippocratic Oath), which continues to be used by the medical profession as a guide to appropriate conduct. The oath is a pledge doctors make to always use their knowledge and best judgment for the benefit of their patients, and to never harm or injure those in their care.

For a brief period after Hippocrates' death, two Greek physician-scholars living in Alexandria, Herophilus and Erasistratus, performed the first known systematic dissections of human bodies. They dissected virtually every organ, including the brain, and recorded what they learned. Despite their dedication to the science of anatomy, these pioneers had little influence on the subsequent practice of medicine. By 150 BCE, dissection of human cadavers was banned throughout the Hellenistic world. Any writings that Herophilus and Erasistratus left behind were lost when Alexandria's library was destroyed in the 3rd century CE.

Among those trained in Hippocratic medicine was Galen (129–216? CE), a Greek who traveled widely and became the most renowned physician in Rome. Although Galen accepted and embellished the four-humors doctrine, he also made important discoveries. He performed systematic experiments on animals (including apes, monkeys, dogs, pigs, snakes, and lions), which involved both dissection and vivisection. He treated gladiators and took advantage of the opportunity to study the internal organs and muscles of the wounded. Galen recognized connections between bodily structures and functions; for example, he demonstrated that a severed spinal cord led to paralysis. He recognized that the heart circulated blood through the arteries but did not understand that it circulated in only one direction. Galen produced a prodigious body of medical scholarship that was followed by medical practitioners for 1,600 years. Unfortunately, his mistaken beliefs were perpetuated alongside his accurate insights.

ARABIAN MEDICINE

After the breakup of the Roman Empire, the tradition of Greek medicine continued in the universities of the Arab world. The Persian physician Al-Razi, or Rhazes (*c.* 854–925/935), is credited with being the first to distinguish between the highly contagious viral diseases smallpox and measles. He also recognized the need for sanitation in hospitals. Probably the most important physician at the beginning

Avicenna in a woodcut illustration from *Liber chronicarum* (*Nuremberg Chronicle*), a book published in 1493

of the second millennium was Avicenna. His monumental *Canon of Medicine*, a five-volume encyclopedia of case histories and therapeutic instructions, was long considered an absolute medical authority in both Eastern and Western traditions.

MEDICINE IN MEDIEVAL AND RENAISSANCE EUROPE

At about the same time that Arabian medicine flourished, the first medical school in Europe was established at Salerno, in southern Italy. Although the school produced no outstanding practitioners or medical discoveries, it was the foremost medical institution of its time. In about 1200 Salerno yielded its place as the premier medical school of Europe to Montpellier, in France. Other great medieval medical schools were founded at Paris, France, and at Bologna and Padua, in Italy.

Even with the presence of these institutions, medicine progressed very slowly in Europe during the Middle Ages. Medieval physicians continued to rely upon ancient medical theories, including that of the humors. They analyzed symptoms, examined waste matter, and made their diagnoses. As treatment, they

might prescribe diet, rest, sleep, exercise, or baths; for some cases they would administer emetics and laxatives, or bleed the patient. Surgeons could treat fractures and dislocations, repair hernias, and perform amputations and a few other operations. Some of them prescribed opium or alcohol to deaden pain. Childbirth was left to midwives, who relied on folklore and tradition.

The Christian church also influenced European medicine during the Middle Ages. It is sometimes said that the early church had a negative effect on medical progress. Disease was regarded as a punishment for sin, and healing required only prayer and repentance. A number of saints became associated with miraculous cures of certain diseases, such as St. Vitus for chorea, a neurological disorder that was termed St. Vitus's dance, and St. Anthony for the skin infection erysipelas, which came to be called St. Anthony's fire. The human body was held sacred and dissection was forbidden during the Middle Ages. Nevertheless, the medieval church played an important role in caring for the sick. Great hospitals were established during this period by religious foundations, and infirmaries were attached to abbeys, monasteries, priories, and convents. Doctors and nurses in these institutions were members of religious orders and combined spiritual with physical healing.

It was not until the Renaissance that Europeans began to seek a truly scientific basis for medical knowledge instead of relying on ancient teachings. The Flemish physician Andreas Vesalius discovered many new principles of anatomy through dissections, which he compiled in his highly illustrated *Seven Books on the Structure of the Human Body*, published in 1543.

Andreas Vesalius

Ambroise Paré (1510–90), a Frenchman, practiced as an army surgeon and became an expert at treating battlefield wounds. He proved that tying blood vessels was a better method of stopping profuse bleeding than cauterizing them with hot oil or a hot iron—a discovery that spared countless soldiers terrible pain and suffering.

17TH- AND 18TH-CENTURY MEDICINE

Based on painstaking observations of his own veins and study of the blood vessels of sheep, English physician William Harvey determined that blood was pumped away from the heart via the arteries and was returned to it by way of the veins. Groundbreaking as this discovery was, Harvey could not explain how blood passed from the arteries to the veins. Four years after Harvey's death in 1657, the Italian researcher Marcello Malpighi, with the aid of a microscope, identified and described the pulmonary and capillary network that connected small arteries with small veins.

The art of surgery developed in 17th-century England at a time when elsewhere in Europe, operations were being performed mainly by barbers. William Cheselden, a surgeon and anatomist, was known for his swift and skillful operations; it was reported that he could perform a lithotomy (removal of a stone from the urinary bladder) in 54 seconds.

Edward Jenner, an English country physician, noticed that women who milked cows often caught cowpox (a relatively mild illness) but never got the much more virulent human disease smallpox. Based on that observation, he began developing the world's first vaccine. In 1796 Jenner inoculated an eight-year-old boy who had never had smallpox with material taken from cowpox lesions on the hands of a dairymaid. Several weeks later, he exposed the boy to smallpox. No disease developed, demonstrating protection through inoculation.

19TH-CENTURY MEDICINE

Before the mid-1800s surgery had to be performed without anesthesia. Patients may have been given a blow on the head, a dose of opium, or a swig of whiskey or rum—at best, these were minimally effective means of reducing pain. The best surgeons, therefore, were those who completed their work in the least amount of time. Early in the century British and American scientists began experimenting with two pain-numbing substances—nitrous oxide, a gas, and ether, a liquid solvent. In 1846, before a large group of doctors at Massachusetts General Hospital in Boston, William Morton (who did not have a medical degree but had been a dentist's apprentice) demonstrated the use of ether anesthesia in a patient undergoing surgery to remove a tumor from his neck. The

resoundingly successful operation was painless for the patient. Word of this achievement spread quickly, and soon dentists and surgeons on both sides of the Atlantic were using anesthesia. In 1847 chloroform was introduced and became the anesthetic of choice.

Certainly one of the most important advances of the 19th century was the development and acceptance of the "germ theory of disease." In the 1840s Ignaz Semmelweis, a young physician working in a hospital in Vienna, recognized that doctors who performed autopsies and then delivered babies were responsible for spreading puerperal (childbed) fever, an often deadly infection of the reproductive organs. After Semmelweis ordered doctors to wash their hands with a chlorinated lime solution before entering the maternity ward, deaths from puerperal fever greatly decreased.

French chemist and microbiologist Louis Pasteur first learned about germs by studying the fermentation of beer, wine, and milk. He went on to explore infectious diseases in farm animals and develop vaccines against anthrax in sheep, erysipelas in swine, and chicken cholera in poultry. Finally Pasteur turned his attention to rabies in humans. His development of a vaccine against the always-fatal viral infection caused by bites of rabid animals was the crowning achievement of Pasteur's career. In 1885 he was urged by doctors to give his experimental vaccine, which had only been tested in dogs, to a young boy who had been bitten more than a dozen times by a rabid dog. Pasteur administered a series of 13 daily injections of increasingly virulent material obtained from the spinal cords of rabid rabbits. The child endured the prolonged and painful treatment and made a full recovery.

German physician Robert Koch discovered that dormant anthrax spores could remain in the blood of sheep for years and, under the right

French chemist and microbiologist Louis Pasteur experimenting on a chloroformed rabbit, colored wood engraving, 1885

conditions, develop into the infectious organisms that caused deadly anthrax outbreaks. In 1876, when he presented his findings on the anthrax disease cycle to doctors in Breslau, Germany, an eminent pathologist commented: "I regard it as the greatest discovery ever made with bacteria and I believe that this is not the last time that this young Robert Koch will surprise and shame us by the brilliance of his investigations." He was right—Koch went on to discover the bacteria responsible for tuberculosis (1882) and human cholera (1883) and to do groundbreaking research on leprosy, plague, and malaria.

In 1880, the French microbiologist Charles Louis Alphonse Laveran discovered the disease-causing protozoan *Plasmodium*, the mosquito-borne parasite responsible for malaria. At the turn of the 20th century, the American army doctor Walter Reed headed a team of physicians who proved that yellow fever also was transmitted by mosquitoes.

The first serious studies of mental illness were conducted during the 19th century. Jean Charcot, a French medical scientist who helped establish the field of modern neurology, used hypnosis as a tool to search the troubled minds of mental patients. His student Sigmund Freud expanded on Charcot's work, and developed the technique of psychoanalysis for treating mental illness.

20TH- AND 21ST-CENTURY MEDICINE

In 1900 the average life expectancy of persons born in the United States was 47 years; by the end of the century it was 77 years. The U.S. Centers for Disease Control and Prevention (CDC) attributed 25 of those 30 additional years of life that Americans had gained to 10 momentous 20th-century public health achievements:

- control of infectious diseases
- immunizations
- decline in deaths from heart disease and stroke
- safer and healthier foods
- healthier mothers and babies
- increased safety of motor vehicles
- safer workplaces
- family planning
- fluoridation of drinking water
- recognition of tobacco use as a health hazard

Triumphs and Challenges in Antibiotic Therapy

Paul Ehrlich's discovery in 1910 of Salvarsan, the first drug effective against syphilis, inaugurated the era of modern antimicrobial drug therapy. The sulfa drugs, which provided strong protection against streptococci and other bacteria, were introduced in the 1930s. In 1938 Ernst Chain and Howard Florey succeeded in synthesizing and purifying the *Penicillium* mold that Alexander Fleming had discovered 10 years earlier; their product, the broad-spectrum antibiotic penicillin, is still widely used today. In 1948 Selman Waksman discovered streptomycin, a powerful antibiotic that led to the control of tuberculosis.

By the late 20th century, however, many commonly used antimicrobial drugs had become increasingly ineffective, allowing the return of previously conquered diseases and the emergence of virulent new infections. By 2007 about five percent of the nine million new cases of tuberculosis in the world each year were resistant to at least two of the four standard drugs; treatment with other drugs was 200 times more expensive and had lower cure rates. In 2007 the CDC reported that the bacterium methicillin-resistant *Staphylococcus aureus* (MRSA) was responsible for more than 90,000 serious infections and 19,000 deaths in the United States annually. For years MRSA had been a problem in health care institutions such as hospitals, nursing homes, and dialysis centers, where it had grown increasingly resistant to commonly used antibiotics. Formerly it primarily infected people with weakened immune systems; by 2007, however, 13 percent of cases were occurring in healthy people living in the community.

THE FIGHT AGAINST DIABETES

In the early 1920s researchers Frederick Banting and Charles Best isolated the hormone insulin, which they used to save the lives of young people with diabetes mellitus. At the time, diabetes mainly affected children and adolescents; because their bodies did not produce insulin, which the body needs to convert food into energy, they died. Shortly after the triumphant work of Banting and Best, the pharmaceutical manufacturer Eli Lilly and Company began large-scale production of cow and pig insulin, which helped turn what is now called Type 1, or insulin-dependent, diabetes from a fatal disease into a manageable disorder that allowed young people to live into

adulthood. Type 2, or insulin-independent, diabetes (in which the body is unable to properly utilize the insulin it produces), remains a challenge to medical science, however. By the end of the century, this form of diabetes had become a public health threat of epidemic proportions; 3.8 million people worldwide died from its complications each year.

IMMUNIZATION AND THE ERADICATION OF DISEASES

The eradication of smallpox, one of the most deadly and debilitating scourges the world had ever known, represents one of the greatest accomplishments in modern medicine, science, and public health. Thanks to widespread vaccination, smallpox was eliminated from Europe, North America, Australia, and New Zealand by 1950 and from most of South and Central America by 1959. In 1967 the World Health Organization (WHO) launched a campaign to eradicate the disease, which still infected up to 15 million people annually in 31 countries. Ten years later, the last case of smallpox was diagnosed in a young man in Somalia, and in 1980 WHO declared smallpox eradicated from the planet. Because humans were the only natural reservoir of the

Patients stand on line at the Clinic Indigène Publique in Mbandaka (formerly Coquilhatville), Congo, waiting to be vaccinated against smallpox in 1963.

smallpox virus, once it was gone, people no longer needed to be vaccinated against it. The only remaining specimens of the virus were retained in high-security laboratories in the United States and Russia.

A global polio eradication initiative was begun in 1988, at which time about 350,000 children in 125 countries on five continents

were crippled each year by the highly contagious viral disease, which attacks the nervous system. By 1999 the number of cases had been reduced by 99 percent, and by the end of 2006, only four countries—India, Nigeria, Pakistan, and Afghanistan—still had endemic polio (uninterrupted transmission of the wild polio virus). Continuing efforts reduced the number of cases to just 222 in 2012, and the campaign's sponsors (WHO, the United Nations Children's Fund, CDC, and Rotary International) expressed confidence that a polio-free world could be achieved by 2018.

THE RISE OF AIDS

The early 1980s saw the emergence of a deadly new disease—acquired immunodeficiency syndrome (AIDS). Caused by the human immunodeficiency virus (HIV), AIDS rapidly grew into a global pandemic. Thanks to the development of life-prolonging drugs, by the mid-1990s HIV/AIDS was no longer a death sentence in wealthy countries. In poor countries, however, the pandemic continued to wreak havoc. In 2001 more than 28 million people in sub-Saharan Africa were living with HIV/AIDS, but fewer than 40,000 had access to drug treatment. At the same time, much of

Africa and many developing countries were profoundly affected by malaria and tuberculosis. These three pandemic diseases killed more than six million people every year.

In 2002 the Global Fund to Fight AIDS, Tuberculosis and Malaria was created to dramatically increase resources to combat the trio of devastating diseases. By mid-2008 the fund had distributed $6.2 billion to 136 countries. At least 1.75 million people were receiving drug treatment for HIV/AIDS, 3.9 million were receiving tuberculosis treatment, and 59 million insecticide-treated mosquito nets had been distributed to families in malaria-ridden countries. The program estimated it had saved more than 1.5 million lives. By 2014 HIV/AIDS still affected more than 24 million people in sub-Saharan Africa; however four in ten people (roughly 37 percent) with HIV/AIDS in the region had access to antiretroviral treatment—a substantial increase from just a decade prior.

GENETICS IN MEDICINE

In 1953 British graduate student Francis Crick and American research fellow James Watson identified the double-helix structure of DNA, a discovery that helped explain how genetic

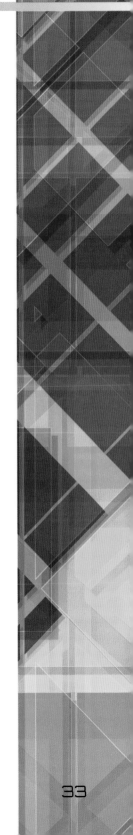

information is passed along. Exactly 50 years later, the Human Genome Project was completed. The 13-year international collaboration of more than 2,800 researchers, one of the boldest scientific undertakings in history, identified all human genes (about 22,000) and determined the sequences of the 3 billion chemical base pairs that make up human DNA. The genetic information provided by the project has enabled researchers to pinpoint errors in genes that cause or contribute to disease. In the future, having the tools to know the precise genetic make-up of individuals will enable clinicians to deliver truly personalized medicine.

As an increasing number of genetic tests have become commercially available—some of which can be lifesaving—new ethical questions have been raised about the best ways to deliver them and how the genetic information they provide should be used by insurers, employers, courts, schools, adoption agencies, and the military. In response to those concerns, in 2008 the U.S. Congress passed and President George W. Bush signed into law the Genetic Information Nondiscrimination Act, which prohibits insurance companies and employers from discriminating on the basis of information derived from genetic tests.

CHAPTER 2

MAJOR BRANCHES OF MEDICINE

At the start of World War II (1939–45) several major medical specialties could be recognized. These included internal medicine, obstetrics and gynecology, pediatrics, pathology, anesthesiology, ophthalmology, surgery, orthopedic surgery, plastic surgery, psychiatry, neurology, radiology, and urology. Hematology was also an important field of study. Advancements in microbiology and biochemistry were especially useful to medical science.

Since World War II, there has been an exponential increase of knowledge in the medical sciences. These developments, coupled with advances in technology, have led to increased specialization. The development of electron microscopy greatly contributed to advances in pathology and hematology. Microbiology, which includes bacteriology, expanded with growth of other subfields such as virology (the study of viruses) and mycology (the study of yeasts and fungi). Advances in biochemistry have

greatly contributed to knowledge of disease, especially with respect to genetics.

Further important contributions to medicine have come from such fields as psychology and sociology, especially in such areas as mental disorders and mental handicaps. More recently established medical specialties are those of preventive medicine, physical medicine and rehabilitation, family practice, and nuclear medicine. Alternative, or complementary, medical practices, such as acupuncture, have also become increasingly available.

This expansion of medical knowledge has encouraged the development of new forms of treatment that require high degrees of specialization. To provide more efficient service it is not uncommon for a specialist surgeon and a specialist physician to form a team that works together to cure and treat ailments. Such a team-based approach brings together a highly trained group of nurses, technologists, operating room technicians, and so on, thus greatly improving the efficiency of the service to the patient.

This chapter examines the main branches of medical practice. Surgery, the branch of medicine that treats injuries and disorders by instrumental means, is examined separately in a later chapter.

CARDIOLOGY

Cardiology is the medical specialty that diagnoses and treats diseases of the heart and blood vessels. Cardiologists care for patients with cardiovascular disease. A cardiologist performs basic studies of heart function and supervises all aspects of therapy, including administration of drugs to modify heart functions.

In 1628 an English physician named William Harvey published his observations on the anatomy (structure) and physiology (function) of the heart and circulation. Harvey's work laid the foundation for the modern field of cardiology. From that time, knowledge grew steadily as physicians used scientific observation, rather than myth and superstition, to study the heart and blood vessels. During the 18th and 19th centuries physicians gained a deeper understanding of the workings of the cardiovascular system: the roles of pulse and blood pressure, and of heart sounds and heart murmurs (thanks largely to the invention of the stethoscope), to name just a few.

Much of cardiology's progress in the 20th century was made possible by improved diagnostic tools. Electrocardiography (the measurement of electrical activity in the heart)

evolved from research by Dutch physiologist Willem Einthoven in 1903. Radiological evaluation of the heart grew out of German physicist Wilhelm Conrad Röntgen's experiments with X-rays in 1895. Echocardiography (the generation of images of the heart by directing ultrasound waves through the chest wall) was introduced in the early 1950s. Cardiac catheterization opened the way for measuring pressure inside the heart, studying normal and abnormal electrical activity, and directly visualizing the heart chambers and blood vessels

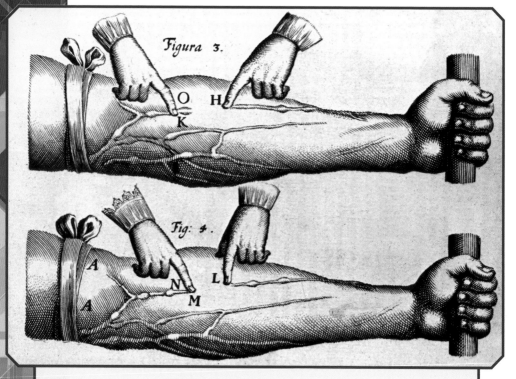

Woodcut depicting William Harvey's theory of the circulation of blood, from his *Exercitatio Anatomica de Motu Cordis et Sanguinis in Animalibus* (1628)

(angiography). Today nuclear cardiology provides a means of measuring blood flow and contraction in heart muscle through the use of radioisotopes.

Treatment options for cardiovascular conditions have also expanded. Drugs are now available to treat a variety of heart-related problems including heart failure, high blood pressure, and arrhythmia, among others. Furthermore, surgeons have developed techniques for allowing the blood circulation to bypass the heart through heart-lung machines, paving the way for surgeries to treat all types of heart diseases. Other advances include heart monitors, pacemakers and defibrillators for detecting and treating arrhythmias, and balloon angioplasty and other nonsurgical treatments of blood clots.

ENDOCRINOLOGY

Endocrinology is the medical branch dealing with the role of hormones and other biochemical factors in regulating bodily functions. Endocrinologists also deal with treatment of hormone imbalances. Although some endocrine diseases, such as diabetes mellitus, have been known since ancient times, endocrinology itself is a fairly recent medical field.

In 1841 German physician Friedrich Henle was the first to recognize "ductless glands," glands that release their products into the bloodstream instead of through specialized ducts. In 1855 French physiologist Claude Bernard named these products "internal secretions," to distinguish them from substances released from other types of glands.

The first endocrine therapy was attempted in 1889 by Mauritian physiologist Charles Brown-Séquard. He used extracts from animal testes to treat male aging, sparking an interest in "organotherapies." In 1902 secretin (produced by the small intestine to trigger the release of pancreatic juices) became the first hormone to be purified. One of its discoverers, English physician Ernest Starling, later applied the term "hormone" to such chemicals in 1905. Starling proposed that this chemical regulation of the body's processes operated in conjunction with control by the nervous system. This concept laid the foundation of modern endocrinology.

The early 20th century saw the purification of a number of other hormones—including thyroxine (1914) and insulin (1921)—leading to new therapies for patients affected by hormonal disorders. The availability of nuclear technology after World War II further led to new treatments for endocrine disorders. The use of radioactive iodine to treat hyperthyroidism was notable in that it greatly reduced the need for thyroid surgery.

GASTROENTEROLOGY

Gastroenterology is concerned with the digestive system and its diseases. Gastroenterologists diagnose and treat the diseases and disorders of the esophagus, stomach, intestines, liver, biliary tract, and pancreas. Among the most common disorders they must deal with are gastroesophageal reflux disease (GERD), gastric and duodenal ulcers, malignant tumors, inflammatory bowel diseases, colorectal cancer, and rectal disorders.

Flemish physician Jan Baptist van Helmont performed the first scientific studies of the digestive system in the 17th century. In 1833 American surgeon William Beaumont's study of a patient shed new light on the nature of gastric juice and the digestive process in general.

A major advance in treatment in the 19th century was the use of gastric lavage (washing out of the stomach) to treat stomach poisoning. This became a standard treatment for all forms of gastric irritation. The long tube

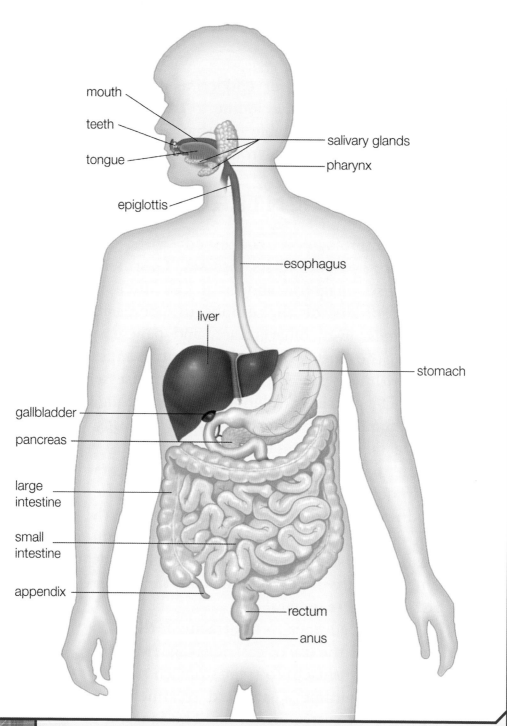

mouth

teeth

tongue

salivary glands

pharynx

epiglottis

esophagus

liver

stomach

gallbladder

pancreas

large intestine

small intestine

appendix

rectum

anus

The human digestive system as seen from the front

used to introduce the lavage fluid was also adapted to view the stomach for diagnostic use. Increasingly sophisticated gastroscopes (instruments for viewing the interior of the stomach) were subsequently developed.

IMMUNOLOGY

Immunology is the scientific study of the body's resistance to invasion by other organisms. In a medical sense, immunology deals with the body's system of defense against disease-causing microorganisms and with disorders in that system's functioning.

The concept of immunology has been known at least since Edward Jenner used cowpox injections to protect people from smallpox in 1796, providing the first vaccinations. But the scientific basis for immunology was not established until a century later. At that point, it was recognized that: (1) the spread of microorganisms in the body was the cause of many infectious diseases, and (2) the body has chemical and cellular components that recognize and destroy foreign substances within it. This new understanding led to successful techniques of immunization that mobilized and stimulated the body's natural defenses against infectious disease.

In the 20th century, immunologists gained an in-depth understanding of the workings of the immune system at the chemical and cellular level. Modern immunology, besides basic techniques such as vaccination, has become highly sophisticated in its manipulation of the body's immune system through drugs and other agents to achieve a desired therapeutic goal.

Advanced immunosuppressive techniques —treatments that suppress the immune system when it has an undesirable reaction—have helped in treating allergies. (An allergy is the immune system's response to the presence of harmless "invaders" such as pollen grains.) Immunosuppressive techniques also have greatly improved the success of bone grafts and organ transplants, which normally would stimulate a immune response and subsequent rejection by the host.

Immunology also includes the study of

Edward Jenner

autoimmune diseases, in which the body's immune system attacks some constituent of its own tissues as if it were a foreign body. The study of immune deficiencies has become an area of intensive research since the appearance of AIDS (acquired immune deficiency syndrome), a disease that destroys the body's immune system.

INTERNAL MEDICINE

Internal medicine is the medical specialty that deals with the diagnosis and medical treatment of diseases of adults. (The treatment of diseases in children is the focus of pediatrics.) As its name implies, internal medicine is a medical, not a surgical, branch of medical science. Internal medicine deals with the entire patient rather than a particular organ system. It is, in effect, the parent of all other medical specialties. Advanced practitioners of internal medicine are called internists.

The development of internal medicine as a medical specialty began with British physician Thomas Sydenham's concept of disease, developed in the 17th century. Sydenham closely observed patients and conceived for the first time the possibility of a variety of

distinct "diseases," as opposed to general illness caused by the imbalance of "humors." His work created a framework for the classification of diseases. In 1763 French physician François Boissier de Sauvages built upon this framework, publishing the first methodical description of disease symptoms. Sauvages emphasized the study of symptoms as the basis for classification of diseases.

From Sauvages' time until the 20th century, internists could do little to treat diseases. Only with the development of disease-specific therapies at the beginning of the 20th century did internal medicine become effective in the cure, rather than just the care, of patients. As more specific medications and treatments became available, more subspecialties devoted to particular organ systems arose. Gradually internal medicine evolved into the specialty of physicians dealing with all problems of the adult patient.

NEPHROLOGY

The study of the kidney and its diseases is the focus of nephrology. The first scientific observations of the kidney were made in the mid-17th century. However, a true understanding of the kidney began with German physiologist Carl Ludwig, who in 1844

46

COMPLEMENTARY AND ALTERNATIVE MEDICINE

Complementary and alternative medicine (CAM) comprises a variety of approaches to human health care that are not part of conventional, or Western, medicine. Some forms of CAM are used to complement standard medical practices. In some instances, however, CAM may be used in place of conventional medicine. Some forms of CAM are referred to as holistic or traditional medicine. The holistic disciplines, such as Ayurvedic medicine and traditional Chinese medicine, are centered on bringing together the mind, body, and spirit. Ayurvedic medicine, which originated in India some 3,000 years ago, incorporates the use of herbal medicines, exercises, and proper diet to achieve health. Traditional Chinese medicine, a system of medicine at least 23 centuries old, relies on the use of acupuncture and Chinese herbal remedies to prevent or heal disease. Less traditional forms of CAM include chiropractic medicine, biofeedback, art therapy, hypnosis, prayer, specialty diets, and therapeutic touch. Many CAM practices are not typically prescribed by physicians who practice conventional medicine. However, the growing evidence that supports the safety and efficacy of certain CAM approaches such as acupuncture has led some conventional medical practitioners to incorporate these modalities in their treatment plans.

proposed the connection between blood pressure and the removal of waste fluids by the kidneys. In 1899, Ernest Starling further

explained the kidney's function by proposing that urine was concentrated there.

Clinical nephrology, the treatment of kidney diseases, emerged as more knowledge was gained about kidney functions. Despite increased information, however, there was little that could be done to treat patients with severe renal (kidney) disease before the 1950s. The first artificial kidney capable of removing blood impurities by the process of dialysis (also called hemodialysis) was developed during World War II. Dialysis works by removing blood from a patient whose kidneys are not functioning (and thereby cannot remove wastes from the blood), purifying that blood by removing wastes, and returning the blood to the patient's body.

Although its development was a tremendous advance, the first artificial kidney could be used only for temporary, reversible renal collapse. In 1960 U.S. physician Belding Scribner created a permanent device—known as the Scribner shunt—that could be used for repeated dialysis for chronic renal disease. The outlook for patients with kidney disease changed from certain death to 90-percent survival. The long-range prospects for these patients was further enhanced by the development of kidney transplants, first successfully performed in the 1950s.

NEUROLOGY

Neurology comprises the branch of medicine that studies the nervous system and its disorders. Neurologists diagnose and treat diseases and disorders of the brain, spinal cord, and nerves.

The first scientific studies of nerve function in animals were performed in the early 18th century by English physiologist Stephen Hales and Scottish physiologist Robert Whytt. Knowledge was gained in the late 19th century about several disorders, including epilepsy and motor problems arising from brain damage, and also about the workings of the brain and nervous functions. French neurologist Jean-Martin Charcot and English neurologist William Gowers described and classified many diseases of the nervous system. The mapping of the functional areas of the brain through selective electrical stimulation also began in the 19th century.

In the 1920s Hans Berger invented the electroencephalograph (EEG), a device that records electrical brain activity. The EEG and new techniques such as the spinal tap (a procedure that removes cerebrospinal fluid from the spinal cord) let neurologists more precisely diagnose and

treat nervous system disorders. The diagnosis and treatment of brain disorders were further advanced by the development of computerized axial tomography (CT) scanning in the early 1970s and magnetic resonance imaging (MRI) in the 1980s. Both techniques gave neurologists detailed, non-invasive views of the inside of the brain.

The identification of chemical agents in the central nervous system and increased understanding of their roles in sending and blocking nerve impulses have led to the introduction of medications that can correct or alleviate many neurological disorders, including Parkinson disease, multiple sclerosis, and epilepsy. Neurosurgery has also benefited from CT scanning and other increasingly precise methods of locating lesions and abnormalities in nervous tissues.

OBSTETRICS AND GYNECOLOGY

Obstetrics and gynecology together form the medical specialty concerned with the care of women from pregnancy until after delivery and with the diagnosis and treatment of disorders of the female reproductive tract.

The medical care of pregnant women (obstetrics) and of female genital diseases

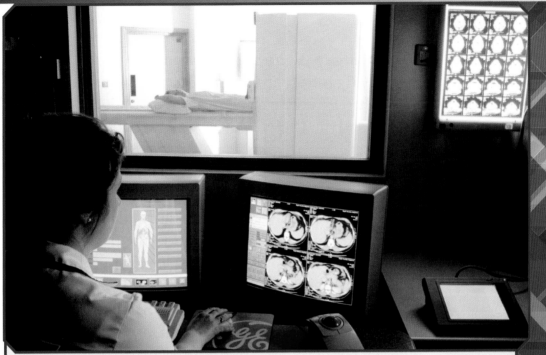

During magnetic resonance imaging (MRI), a patient lies inside a hollow cylindrical magnet and is exposed to a powerful magnetic field.

(gynecology) developed along different historical paths. Childbirth had for a long time been handled by female midwives. In the 17th century, however, European physicians began to attend on normal deliveries of royal and upper class families. The practice then spread to the middle classes. A series of major advances such as the invention of the forceps used in delivery and the use of antiseptics methods transformed obstetrics. The use of antiseptic methods made cesarean section, in which the infant is delivered through an incision in the mother's uterus and abdominal wall, a

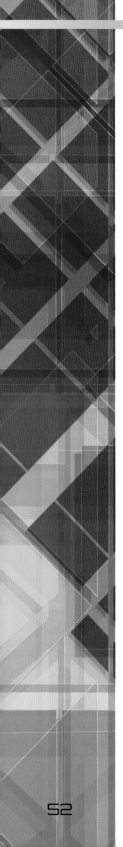

feasible surgical alternative to natural childbirth. By the early 19th century, obstetrics had become established as a recognized medical discipline in Europe and the United States.

In the 20th century, obstetrics mainly advanced in the areas of birth control and the promotion of healthy births. Prenatal care to reduce birth defects and problem deliveries became commonplace about 1900. The development of hormonal contraceptive pills in the 1950s greatly advanced the regulation of women's fertility, as have developments in artificial insemination (which have helped previously infertile couples have children). New methods have also developed for the prenatal detection of birth defects.

The obstetrician's main tasks are to diagnose and bring a woman through pregnancy, deliver her child, and give the new mother adequate postnatal care. The gynecologist, in contrast, is concerned with the general health of the female reproductive tract. To this end, gynecologists make routine examinations to detect cancer of the reproductive organs, and also may perform certain surgeries.

Gynecology as a branch of medicine dates back to Greco-Roman civilization, if not earlier. In the early and mid-19th century, physicians became able to successfully perform specific surgical operations on the ovaries and uterus. However, pioneers of gynecology had to combat strong prejudice against exposure or examination of the female sexual organs. The two great advances that helped end such opposition and make gynecologic surgery generally available were the use of anesthesia and antiseptic methods. Gynecology as a medical specialty became well established by 1880. Late in the 19th century came its union with obstetrics, which continues to the present day.

OPHTHALMOLOGY

The field of ophthalmology deals with the diagnosis and treatment of diseases and disorders of the eye. The first ophthalmologists were called oculists. These paramedical specialists practiced on a traveling basis during the Middle Ages. Georg Bartisch, a German physician who studied eye diseases in the 16th century, is sometimes credited with founding ophthalmology.

Oculists were the first to develop many important eye operations, including the surgical correction of strabismus (a disorder in which the eyes are misaligned), which was first performed in 1738. The first descriptions of visual defects included those of glaucoma

(1750), night blindness (1767), color blindness (1794), and astigmatism (1801).

In 1864 advances in optics by the Dutch physician Frans Cornelis Donders established the modern system of prescribing and fitting eyeglasses. The invention of the ophthalmoscope, which allowed ophthalmologists to look at the interior of the eye, made it possible to relate eye defects to internal medical conditions.

In the 20th century, advances in ophthalmology mainly involved the prevention of eye disease through regular eye exams and the early treatment of eye defects. Another major development was the eye bank, first established in 1944 in New York, which increased the availability of corneal tissue for eye transplants.

Optometry is a related field that is concerned with the examination of the eyes to diagnose vision problems, eye diseases, or other abnormalities. Unlike ophthalmologists, who are medical doctors with a specialization in eye diseases, optometrists are not usually licensed to prescribe drugs or trained to perform surgery.

OTOLARYNGOLOGY

Otolaryngology is the medical specialty concerned with the diagnosis and treatment of diseases of the ear, nose, and throat.

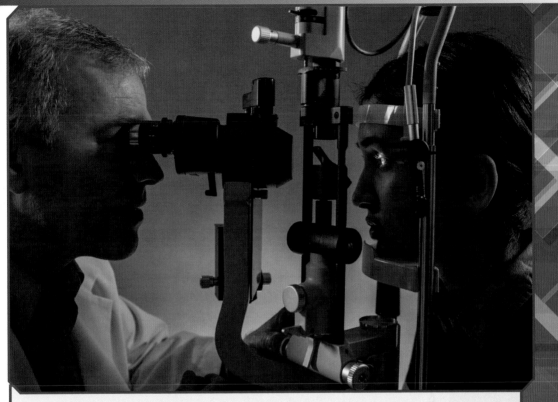

An eye doctor uses a slit lamp to closely examine a patient's eye.

Traditionally, treatment of the ear was associated with that of the eye in medical practice. With the development of laryngology in the late 19th century, the connection between the ear and throat became known, and otologists (doctors of the ear) became associated with laryngologists (doctors of the throat).

The study of ear diseases did not develop a scientific basis until the first half of the 19th century, when French physicians Jean-

Marc-Gaspard Itard and Prosper Ménière made ear physiology and disease a matter of systematic investigation. Irish eye and ear surgeon William R. Wilde published the first scientific accounts of the specialty in 1853. Further advances were made with the development of the otoscope, an instrument that allowed for visual examination of the eardrum.

The investigation of the larynx (voice box) and its diseases, meanwhile, was aided by a device invented in 1855 by Manuel García, a Spanish singing teacher. This instrument, the laryngoscope, was adopted by Austrian neurologist Ludwig Türck and Austrian-German physiologist Johann Czermak, who studied the functioning of the larynx. Czermak also turned the laryngoscope's mirror upward to study the functioning of the nasopharyngeal (nose-throat) cavity, establishing an essential link between the study of the throat and nose.

In 1921 Swedish otologist Carl Nylen first used a high-powered binocular microscope to perform ear surgery, opening the way to several new corrective procedures. Another important 20th-century achievement was the development in the 1930s of the electric audiometer, an instrument used to measure sharpness of hearing.

PATHOLOGY

Pathology is the medical specialty that studies the causes of disease. It also considers the changes in structure and function that occur in abnormal conditions. Early efforts to study pathology were often blocked by religious bans on autopsies. These prohibitions were relaxed during the late Middle Ages, and autopsies began to be used to determine the cause of death—the basis for pathology. These autopsies led to the publication of the first anatomy textbook in 1761, which located diseases within individual organs for the first time. However, the relationship between clinical symptoms and pathological changes was not made until the 19th century.

Pathology as a medical specialty was fairly well established by the end of the 19th century. Most of the pathologist's work takes place in the laboratory; reports are shared with the clinical physician who directly attends to the patient. Laboratory specimens examined by the pathologist include surgically removed body parts, blood, other bodily fluids such as urine, and feces.

The work of pathologists also includes the reconstruction—through autopsy—of the last chapter of the physical life of a deceased

person. This practice provides valuable (and otherwise unobtainable) information about how diseases work. The knowledge required for practicing pathology is too great to be attainable by single individuals; when possible, specialists work together.

PEDIATRICS

Pediatrics is the medical specialty dealing with the development and care of children and with the diagnosis and treatment of childhood diseases. The specialized focus of pediatrics did not begin to emerge in Europe until the 18th century. At that time the first specialized children's hospitals were opened. These hospitals later became major centers for training in pediatrics, which, by the middle of the 19th century, began to be taught as a separate discipline in medical schools.

The major focus of early pediatrics was the treatment of infectious diseases that affected children. Thomas Sydenham had laid the groundwork for the classification of scarlet fever, measles, and other childhood diseases in the 17th century. Clinical studies of childhood diseases became numerous throughout the 18th and 19th centuries, leading to publication of the first modern textbooks of pediatrics in France in the mid-19th century. However, there was little that could be done to cure childhood diseases until the end of the 19th century.

As childhood diseases came under control through the combined efforts of pediatricians, immunologists, and public-health workers, the focus of pediatrics changed. Early in the 20th century the first children's clinics were established to monitor and study the normal growth of children. By the mid-20th century, the use of antibiotics and vaccines had all but eliminated most serious infectious childhood diseases in the developed world, and infant and child mortality rates fell to the lowest levels ever. In the last half of the century, pediatrics again expanded to incorporate the study of behavioral and social, as well as medical, aspects of child health.

PSYCHIATRY

Psychiatry is the science and practice of diagnosing, treating, and preventing mental disorders. Psychiatrists are medical doctors who have completed a residency in psychiatry. They diagnose mental illness through clinical interviews and psychological tests

and by examining the patient's history. They also study the causes of mental illness and the effectiveness of different treatment procedures.

The practice of clinical psychology is closely aligned with psychiatry. Like psychiatrists, clinical psychologists diagnose and treat mental illness. They are not physicians, however, and cannot prescribe or administer drugs.

Until the 18th century, mental illness was most often seen as demonic possession, but it gradually came to be considered as a sickness requiring treatment. Modern psychiatry is thought to have emerged through the efforts of French physician Philippe Pinel in the late 1700s. His contemporary in the United States, Benjamin Rush, introduced a comparable approach. Perhaps the most significant contributions to the field occurred in the late 19th century, when German psychiatrist Emil Kraepelin emphasized a systematic approach to psychiatric diagnosis and Austrian psychoanalyst Sigmund Freud developed psychoanalysis as a treatment approach.

Certified psychiatrists address the biological sources of mental and emotional disorders through treatments such as drug therapy, electroconvulsive therapy, and biofeedback. In addition, they apply different forms of psychotherapy, such as cognitive, behavioral, or interpersonal psychotherapies, to treat the psychological elements of mental and emotional dysfunction.

Successful psychiatry relies on a combination of different treatments based on the complexities of mind-brain interactions. Developing such treatment involves an understanding of environmental factors and of how these factors apply to individuals with mental illness. Most mental and emotional disorders require such a pluralistic approach to treatment because they affect so many facets of the human experience. As a result, psychiatrists frequently work as part of a multidisciplinary treatment team with psychologists and other therapists or social workers.

The development of technology that allows for measurement and observation of brain function has greatly aided growth in the science of psychiatry. Neuroimaging techniques, such as CT and MRI scans, have begun to answer basic questions about psychopathologic disorders and normal development and function. These technologies are increasingly being used to integrate the different biological, psychological, and sociological dimensions of mental and emotional illness.

UROLOGY

Urology is the medical specialty involving the diagnosis and treatment of diseases and disorders of the urinary tract and of the male reproductive organs. (The urinary tract consists of the kidneys, the bladder, the ureters, and the urethra.)

The modern practice of urology derives directly from the medieval lithologists—traveling healers who specialized in the surgical removal of bladder stones. In 1588 the Spanish surgeon Francisco Díaz wrote the first studies on diseases of the bladder, kidneys, and urethra; he is generally regarded as the founder of modern urology. Most modern urologic procedures appeared during the 19th century, as flexible catheters were developed for examining and draining the bladder. In 1877 German urologist Max Nitze developed the cystoscope, a tubelike viewing instrument equipped with an electric light on its end that allowed practitioners to view the interior of the bladder.

Urologic surgery was largely confined to the removal of bladder stones until the German surgeon Gustav Simon demonstrated in 1869 that human patients could survive the removal of one kidney, as long as the remaining kidney

was healthy. The introduction of various X-ray techniques in the early 20th century proved very useful in diagnosing disorders of the urinary tract.

In addition to the treatment of urinary tract disorders, the urologist also is concerned with the health of the prostate gland. This structure, which encircles the male urethra close to the juncture between the urethra and the bladder, is often the site of cancer. Even more frequently, it grows larger in middle or old age, causing partial or complete obstruction of the flow of urine through the urethra. Urologists treat prostate enlargement either by removing the prostate or by creating a wider passageway through it. Urologists may also operate to remove stones from the urinary tract, and may perform operations to remove cancers of the kidneys, bladder, and testicles.

CHAPTER 3

CLINICAL PRACTICE

Most countries try to organize their health services in a way that ensures that citizens and communities can access and benefit from the latest knowledge and technology. In doing so, governments are faced with many tasks. For one, they must collect information regarding the size and urgency of citizens' medical needs. These needs must then be assessed in relation to the availability of resources, which may be limited by costs or lack of manpower. Developing countries often require foreign aid to supplement their own resources. Based on their findings from these first two tasks, countries then must determine realistic objectives and draw up plans. Finally, governments must evaluate their health-care program. Misinformation or poor use of funds can lead to confusion and inefficiency.

Health services entail a variety of characteristics, among which the most obvious, but not necessarily the most important from a national point of view, is caring for the already ill. Other responsibilities include special services that deal with particular groups (such as children or pregnant women); preventive services, which protect both individual and community health; the collection and analysis of information; and health education.

LEVELS OF HEALTH CARE

In caring for the sick, there are various forms of medical practice. Generally speaking, they can be said to form a pyramid-like structure, with three levels. Moving up the pyramid, there is an increasing degree of specialization and technical sophistication. However moving up the pyramid also reveals fewer patients, as many are filtered out of the health-care system at lower levels.

The first level of the pyramid represents primary health care, or first contact care. This is the level at which patients have their first contact with the health-care system. Only those patients who require special attention (either for diagnosis or treatment) should reach the second (advisory) or third (specialized treatment) levels. At each increasing level, the cost per service becomes higher.

Primary health care is a central part of a country's health maintenance system. It forms the largest and most important part of any health-care system. Most countries aim to make primary health care available to all citizens and communities at a cost that either the country or an individual community can afford to maintain. Primary health care in developed countries is usually administered by medically qualified physicians; in developing countries it is often provided by non-medically qualified personnel.

The vast majority of patients can be fully treated at the primary level. Those who cannot are referred to the second level: secondary health care, or the referral services. At this level, a patient is referred for the opinion of a consultant with specialized knowledge or for X-ray examinations and special tests. Secondary health care often requires the technology offered by a local or regional hospital. Increasingly, however, radiological and laboratory services are available directly to family physicians, improving the services offered to patients and increasing their range.

The third tier of health care employs specialist services. This level of care is offered by institutions such as teaching hospitals and units devoted to the care of particular groups

Decrease in number of patients; Increase in costs

Specialist services

Greater number of patients; Lower costs

Secondary health care (Referral services)

Primary health care (First contact care)

Diagram depicting the three levels of health care

(such as women, children, and patients with mental disorders). The drastic differences in treatment costs at the various levels is of particular importance in developing countries, where costs at the primary health-care level are usually only a small fraction of those at

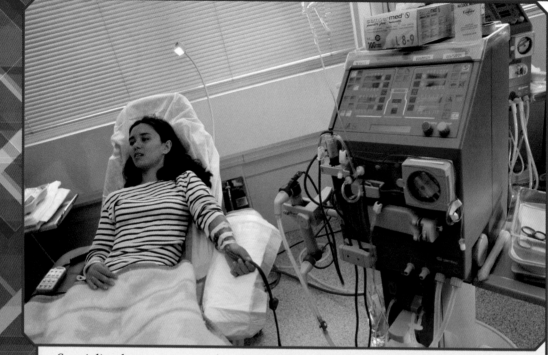

Specialized treatment, such as hemodialysis, generally costs more and must be performed in a hospital or other dedicated facility.

the third level. Nonetheless the government usually bears medical costs at any level in such countries.

Ideally, health care at all levels would be available to all patients. Such health care is termed "universal." The upper classes, both in the developed and the developing world, often have access to medical attention from sources of their choosing and for which they can pay in the private sector. The vast majority of people in most countries, however, are dependent to a degree on state-provided health services, for which these citizens may contribute comparatively little or, in the case of poor countries, nothing at all.

ADMINISTRATION OF PRIMARY HEALTH CARE

In many parts of the world, particularly in developing countries, people get their primary health care from non-medically qualified personnel. Such medical auxiliaries are being trained in increasing numbers to meet overwhelming needs among fast-growing populations. Even among the world's developed countries—which contain a much smaller percentage of the world's population—the rising costs of health services and of physician training have given cause to rethink the role of the medical doctor in delivery of first-contact care.

Nonetheless in advanced industrial countries it is still usually a trained physician who provides first-contact care. The patient seeking this care can go either to a general practitioner or directly to a specialist. Which is the wisest choice has become a subject of some debate. The general practitioner, however, is becoming less common in some developed countries. Where such practitioners do still exist, they are being increasingly seen as archaic figures—a

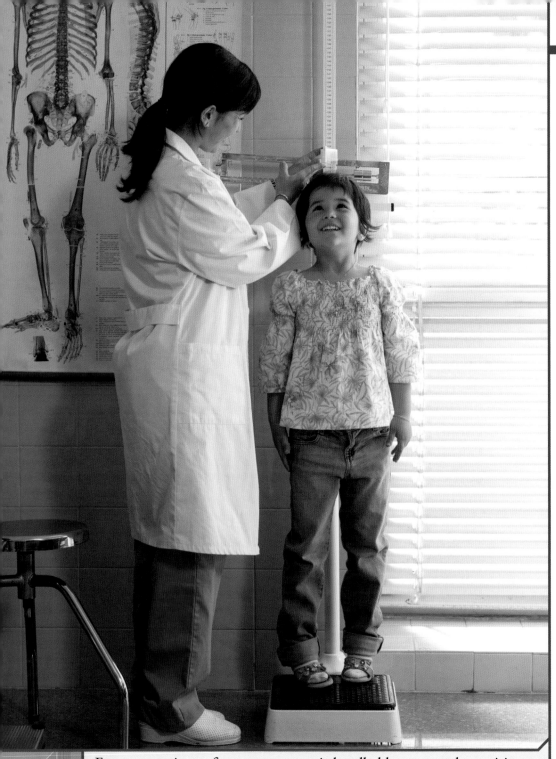

For most patients, first-contact care is handled by a general practitioner. Here, a child meets with her pediatrician, a primary care physician who specializes in the treatment of infants, children, and adolescents.

result of increased specialization in medical science. It is no longer possible for a physician to master more than a small fraction of medicine. The concept of the general practitioner, it is argued, may no longer be useful.

The alternative to general practice is the direct access of a patient to a specialist. If a patient has problems with vision, he or she goes to an eye specialist; for a pain in the chest, the patient goes to a heart specialist. One objection to this model is that patients often cannot know which organ is responsible for their symptoms. Breathlessness—a common symptom—may be due to heart disease, to lung disease, to anemia, or to emotional upset. Another common symptom is general malaise—feeling run-down or always tired. Headache, chronic low backache, stomach discomfort, poor appetite, and constipation also are common complaints. Some patients may feel anxious or depressed.

Among the subtlest medical skills is the ability to assess people with such symptoms and to determine the cause—emotional or bodily—of the ailment. While a specialist may be able to make this assessment, a generalist with his or her broader training is often the better choice for a first diagnosis. Referral to a specialist is then the next option.

Many feel there are also practical advantages to a patient having his or her own doctor, who knows about the patient's background, has seen the patient through various illnesses, and who has often seen the rest of the patient's family as well. This personal physician, often a generalist, is in the best position to decide when the patient should be referred to a consultant.

The advantages of general practice and specialization are combined when the physician of first contact is a pediatrician. Although pediatricians see only children and thus acquire a special knowledge of childhood maladies, they remain generalists who look at the whole patient. Another combination of general practice and specialization is represented by group practice. In group practice, individual doctors work in the same office and each partially or fully works in a specific medical specialty. One or more may be general practitioners; other group members may include a surgeon, an obstetrician, a pediatrician, and an internist. Group practice may be the best option in nonurban areas, where access to medical specialists is difficult. However, in urban regions, where such access is less restricted, it may be preferable to see a specialist at a hospital over a general practitioner in a small office.

WHAT DOCTORS DO

Physicians have several key tasks in the course of serving a patient. The first of these is to make an accurate diagnosis—that is, to identify the exact nature of the problem. Following a proper diagnosis, the physician will select the appropriate course of treatment. Finally the doctor issues a prognosis—a prediction of the probable outcome of the case based on knowledge of the current problem, previous experiences treating it, and the health status of the patient.

DIAGNOSIS

A diagnosis is the process of identifying a disease and its cause. To correctly diagnose a medical problem, doctors first obtain a patient's medical history by asking pertinent questions about current and past health and illnesses, personal habits, lifestyle, family health, and so forth. The history will indicate how and when the patient became sick and whether or not he or she ever previously had the same or a similar condition.

A patient's history will reveal one or more symptoms—body changes that the patient can detect, such as pain, fatigue, loss of appetite, and nausea. Symptoms are clues that help

doctors decide what signs they should look for. (Note that a *symptom* is something a patient can detect, whereas a *sign* is something that a doctor can detect or observe in a patient.) For example, a case of appendicitis would be diagnosed on the basis of a patient's complaints of abdominal pain, appetite loss, nausea, and vomiting (symptoms), which would prompt the physician to check for fever, tenderness in the lower right abdomen, and a high number of white cells in the blood (signs). Together, these symptoms and signs would lead to a diagnosis of probable appendicitis.

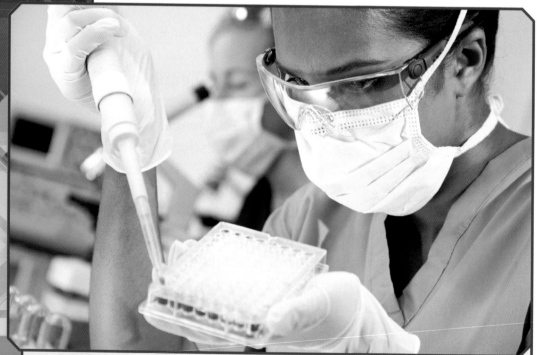

Sometimes, proper diagnosis of a medical problem requires a laboratory examination of blood or tissue samples by a trained technician.

ADVANCED METHODS FOR DIAGNOSIS

While some simple diagnoses can be made on the basis of symptoms and observable signs, physicians often rely on technology or tests to determine a patient's illness. Simple tests, such as analyses of blood or urine, can help to pinpoint many disorders. In some cases, radiographs, or X rays, may be indicated for accurate diagnosis. Electrical graphing tests, such as the electrocardiogram (ECG) or the electroenceph-alogram (EEG), may be indicated. The latter tests, which monitor the electrical activity of the heart and brain, respec-tively, can be performed by the doctor or at a laboratory.

If a genetic disease is suspected, a doctor may be able to confirm the diagnosis with a simple test in the office. However, many genetic tests require laboratory analysis of a blood or tissue sample. Genetic testing can determine if a person is at risk for developing a hereditary disease later in life. It can also be used with prospective parents before or after conception to determine if either is a carrier for a genetic disease.

Some diseases require a surgical diagnosis, such as exploratory surgery or a biopsy. In the latter procedure a small sample of tissue is taken from the patient and exam-ined under a microscope. Simple skin biopsies may be done in a doctor's office; biopsies of deeper tissues, such as the liver, require surgical conditions.

Advances in X-ray technology have enabled highly spe-cific diagnoses of certain problems. Mammography is a special X-ray technique that can detect tumors and other growths in a woman's breast; contrast X rays such as angio-grams are used to examine the circulatory system after a special dye has been injected. Computerized imaging such

CONTINUED ON THE NEXT PAGE

ADVANCED METHODS FOR
DIAGNOSIS (CONTINUED FROM PREVIOUS PAGE)

as CT (computed tomography) scans allow doctors to view cross-sectional images of the body. Other advanced imaging techniques use high-frequency sound waves (ultrasonography) or magnetic fields and radio waves (magnetic resonance imaging, or MRI).

Among the most important diagnostic technologies developed in the late 20th century was the use of fiber-optic imaging. This involves an ultra-thin glass tube with a tiny camera at one end that can be inserted deep into the body to examine tissues and organs previously only viewable with surgery. Today this diagnostic technique is used to examine a wide range of body cavities and structures, including the colon (colonoscopy), esophagus and stomach (endoscopy), and abdomen (laparoscopy), among others.

TREATMENT

After diagnosis, the next task of the physician is to prescribe an appropriate treatment to correct a particular illness in a patient. The clear choice for the patient with appendicitis would be surgery to remove the appendix. A delay in surgery could result in rupture of the appendix and serious infection. Because of the risk of infection during and after the operation, the physician is also likely to prescribe antibiotic therapy.

Increasingly doctors are practicing "evidence-based medicine"—an approach that involves conscientious use of results from well-controlled clinical trials in making treatment decisions. Proponents of evidence-based medicine consider it the most objective way to ensure that patients receive optimal care. In recent years, many specialties have issued detailed "clinical practice guidelines" based on the best evidence available. These compilations enable clinicians to readily choose treatments backed by solid science.

Before a physician proceeds with a treatment, he or she must (by law) convey the details of the planned procedure (including all the risks) to the patient in language the patient comprehends. The patient then must sign an "informed consent" document acknowledging consent of the treatment and full awareness of potential outcomes.

PROGNOSIS

The prognosis is the doctor's prediction of the probable outcome of a case based on knowledge of the disease, previous experiences treating it, and the health status of the patient. When appendicitis strikes an otherwise healthy child, the doctor can usually

Physicians are legally obligated to carefully review their planned course of treatment with a patient so that the patient is aware of risks and possible side effects and may consent to his or her treatment.

make an optimistic prognosis. However, if an obese adult with high blood pressure develops appendicitis that is not diagnosed promptly, the potential for rupture of the appendix and infection is high. Moreover, the patient's excess weight and elevated blood pressure increase the risk of surgical complications. In this case the prognosis would be less certain, as the doctor would not be able to predict how the patient would endure surgery, how extensive infection might be, or how long the healing process would take.

CHAPTER 4

DISEASE AND EPIDEMIOLOGY

Disease can be defined as a condition that impairs the proper function of the body or of one of its parts. All living things can succumb to disease. People, for example, are often infected by bacteria, but bacteria, in turn, can be infected by certain viruses. The branch of medical science that studies the spread of disease in human populations and the factors influencing that spread is termed epidemiology. Public health officials use epidemiology to manage society's response to disease.

Hundreds of different diseases exist in nature, and every disease has a cause, though the causes of some remain to be discovered. Each disease has a particular set of symptoms and signs—the clues that assist in diagnosis. All diseases display a cycle consisting of three main stages: the onset, or beginning of symptoms; the course, or timespan of affliction; and the resolution, or end of the disease. Resolution may occur

when the disease and its signs and symptoms disappears via a cure or through the death of the patient. Some diseases, such as polio, are considered "resolved" even though the victim is left disabled.

How Disease Is Classified

Diseases can be classified in a number of ways, depending on the information needed by the doctor or scientist. Diseases are generally defined as either acute or chronic. An acute disease has a quick onset; most run a relatively short course, during which symptoms may be mild or severe. The common cold is a relatively mild acute disease of fairly short duration. SARS, or severe acute respiratory syndrome, also has a quick onset. However, unlike a cold, SARS can rapidly become very serious, even fatal. A chronic disease has a slow onset and a long duration that can last for years. Rheumatoid arthritis is an example of a chronic ailment with a very long course. Some diseases, such as bronchitis, have both acute and chronic forms.

A key way of classifying diseases is to distinguish between infectious and noninfectious diseases. Infectious diseases are caused by

Children in Hong Kong stand in line wearing masks to protect them against SARS during the 2003 outbreak of that disease.

living organisms such as bacteria, fungi, protozoans, viruses, and parasites. Whatever the causative agent may be, it survives in the host (the individual whose body it has invaded) and is thereby infectious. If it can be passed on to another person, the disease is also communicable. Noninfectious diseases are not caused by a living organism; and because they are not passed from one individual to another, they are noncommunicable. Noninfectious diseases have a wide range of causes, such as substances in the environment (silicosis and black lung), diet deficiencies (rickets and scurvy), immune system disorders (lupus), or inheritable genetic defects (Tay-Sachs disease).

Diseases generally are classified according to the organ or organ system that has been affected. There are diseases of the respiratory system (pneumonia), cardiovascular system (coronary artery disease), nervous system (multiple sclerosis), and endocrine system (diabetes mellitus), among many others.

Diseases and their associated signs and symptoms are further distinguished by the extent of their spread in the body. A local, or localized, ailment or symptom is confined to a particular site or single organ system, whereas a systemic disease affects the entire body. This is an important factor in treatment. For example, an infected cut may be treated with a topical antibiotic cream if the infection is limited to the site of the injury. If the infection invades deeper tissues and spreads to the bloodstream, the infectious organism can be carried to every organ in the body. To treat this, doctors must prescribe a systemic drug; this is usually an oral or injectable medication that can enter the bloodstream and fight the infection at all affected sites. Not all systemic diseases are infectious, however. Cancer and diabetes mellitus are two examples of non-infectious systemic diseases.

INFECTIOUS DISEASES

Humans live in a world where many other living things compete for food and places to breed. Some of these organisms—bacteria, for instance—live within the human body and contribute to bodily functions such as digestion. Ordinarily, the immune system keeps these microbes from causing damage.

Sometimes, however, harmful bacteria penetrate the body's defenses. In other cases, organisms living harmlessly within the body become too numerous or acquire harmful characteristics. They then become pathogenic, or disease-causing, organisms (called pathogens

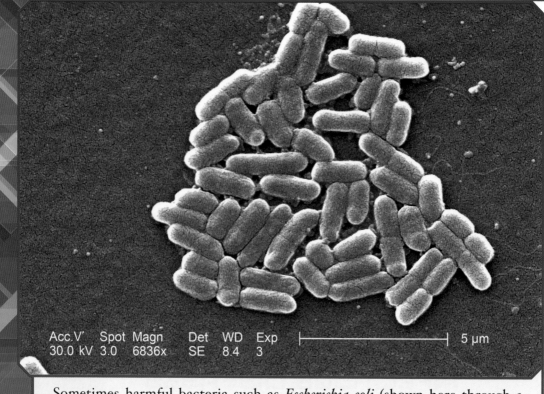

Acc.V′   Spot   Magn   Det   WD   Exp
30.0 kV   3.0   6836x   SE   8.4   3   5 μm

Sometimes harmful bacteria such as *Escherichia coli* (shown here through a microscope) penetrate the body's defenses.

or simply germs). The same is true for fungi, viruses, and parasites.

HOW GERMS INVADE THE BODY

Pathogenic organisms can enter the body in various ways. Some, such as the virus that causes the common cold, are inhaled, while others, such as the bacterium that causes leprosy, enter through direct contact between human bodies. Many pathogens, such as those that cause gastroenteritis (sometimes called stomach flu) get into the body through contaminated food, water, or utensils. Certain pathogens are transmitted only through sexual activity with an infected individual.

Some germs may enter the body through the bite of an animal. Mosquitoes transmit West Nile virus and *Plasmodium*, the parasite that causes malaria. Typhus is caused by infection with rickettsial bacteria transmitted by lice. The microbe that causes Lyme disease is spread through the bite of a tick, while the rabies virus is transmitted via the bite of an infected mammal. Organisms that deliver an infectious agent to a host are called carriers. In many cases, carriers themselves do not become ill. For example, mosquitoes are unaffected by the parasites and viruses they carry. Other diseases, such as rabies, cause illness in carrier and host alike.

To acquire certain contagious diseases, a person need only be in the presence of someone who is already ill, or come in contact with infected bodily fluids such as blood or urine. Infectious diseases are called contagious if they can be passed between people. Anyone suffering the frank symptoms of a contagious disease can pass it on to others while the disease is running its course. However, some pathogens can be transmitted during the incubation period of a disease—the time between infection and the onset of symptoms. Some pathogens can be transmitted when the initial victim is recovering from the disease. Like animals, some people can be asymptomatic carriers, carrying an infectious organism without ever falling ill.

Most infectious diseases are species-specific—that is, a disease such as parvovirus,

A South Korean official monitors the body temperature of passengers arriving at Incheon International Airport during an outbreak of swine flu in 2009. Passengers exhibiting a high temperature were examined and quarantined, as needed, to prevent spreading the disease to others.

which affects dogs, will not affect humans. However, a large number of diseases can strike both humans and animals and can be passed between them (though most commonly these are transmitted from animals to humans and not vice versa). These diseases are called zoonoses. Zoonotic diseases are a public health concern, though some are more serious than others. Ringworm, for example, is relatively mild and can be treated with antifungal drugs. Other zoonoses, such as rabies, avian influenza virus, and plague, are very serious and can lead to epidemics.

Once an infectious organism gains a foothold in the body, it begins to multiply. The length of the incubation period depends on the pathogen. Symptoms of the common cold appear within days, while those of kuru, a rare disease of the nervous system, can appear years after infection.

Several factors determine whether a person will fall ill after being infected. These include the number of invading germs, or the dose of the infection; the body's ability to fight the disease; and the virulence of the pathogen. Virulence is a measure of a pathogen's ability to do harm. Highly virulent pathogens, such as the Ebola virus, cause severe disease that progresses so rapidly that, in most cases,

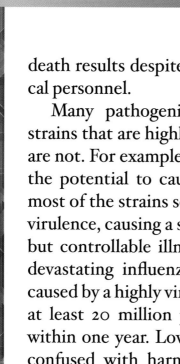

death results despite the best efforts of medical personnel.

Many pathogenic species include some strains that are highly virulent and others that are not. For example, all influenza strains have the potential to cause severe illness, though most of the strains seen each winter are low in virulence, causing a short course of unpleasant but controllable illness in most victims. The devastating influenza pandemic of 1918 was caused by a highly virulent flu strain that killed at least 20 million people around the world within one year. Low virulence should not be confused with harmlessness, however—even organisms with low virulence can cause serious illness if left untreated.

How Infections Are Fought

As a first line of defense, a healthy body has a number of physical barriers against infection. The skin and mucous membranes covering the body and lining its cavities offer considerable resistance to invasion by infectious organisms. If these barriers are injured or burned, however, resistance drops. In that case, the body calls up its second line of defense: the immune system. Circulating through the blood and lymph, white blood cells flock to infected areas and try to localize and suppress the infection. Some white blood cells, such as macrophages, engulf and digest the pathogens in a process known as phagocytosis.

Lymphocytes, another group of white blood cells, play a key role during this line of defense. Lymphocytes are divided into two main classes, or types: T cells and B cells. T cells use several methods to kill pathogens directly, in some cases tagging them with markers so that other cells can attack them. B cells manufacture and release protective proteins called antibodies, which are "custom designed" by the B cells to target specific pathogens. Some B cells remain in the body for years after the pathogen has been eliminated. This creates a biological "memory," giving the body a long-lasting immunity against future attacks by the same kind of invader.

Drug Therapy

Since the advent of antibiotic therapy in the 20th century, a broad range of infection-fighting drugs has been developed to work in conjunction with the body's immune system. The antibiotics penicillin and tetracycline, for instance, are very effective against some bacterial infections, such as gonorrhea and acne.

However, antibiotics have no effect on infections caused by viruses, fungi, protozoa, or other parasites. Thus nonbacterial infectious diseases are treated with other classes of drugs. For example, herpesvirus infections do not respond to antibiotics (because the infection is not caused by bacteria), but some herpesvirus infections respond to the antiviral drug acyclovir. Similarly, antifungal drugs are used to treat fungal infections, antiprotozoal medicines treat diseases caused by infection with protozoa, and anthelmintics fight worm infestations such as trichinosis, which is caused by intestinal roundworms.

Drug Resistance

Some individual microbes are naturally resistant to certain drugs. After repeated exposure to a drug, however, some nonresistant microbes may gain resistance by a chance mutation; other microbes may acquire genes for resistance by mating with a resistant bacterium. Over time these bacteria form a new drug-resistant strain, forcing doctors to prescribe multiple drugs to fight infections with these germs—which may later gain resistance to the new drugs.

Incorrect antibiotic use has led to a rise of drug-resistant pathogens, producing a global

Shown is a penicillin culture. While once highly effective in treating certain infections, overuse of penicillin has led to a rise in drug-resistant pathogens.

public health issue. Once-powerful drugs such as penicillin have become ineffective against newly drug-resistant bacteria strains,

such as those that cause tuberculosis and staphylococcal infections. As a result, the incidence of these once-controllable diseases is steadily increasing.

VACCINES

Many dangerous diseases have been controlled or eradicated (stamped out) through the use of vaccines. Some vaccines protect against viruses, such as measles; others guard against some bacterial infections, such as diphtheria, or toxins, such as tetanus. The once-widespread viral disease called smallpox was eradicated around the world in the 20th century, thanks to an international effort aimed at wide-scale vaccination.

EPIDEMIOLOGY

The focus of epidemiology is to control the spread of and, where possible, to eradicate disease. Epidemiologists seek to classify diseases by the population groups they affect and by the way they spread.

Unlike other medical disciplines, epidemiology concerns itself with populations, or groups of people, rather than individuals. It developed in the 19th century out of the search for causes of human disease—especially of epidemic outbreaks. One of its chief functions remains the identification of populations at high risk for a given disease, so that the cause may be identified and preventive measures begun.

EPIDEMIC

When a disease occurs in a high number of people in a population, an epidemic is said to exist. An epidemic occurring over a wide area is called a pandemic. For an infectious disease, its prevalence—the number of cases existing at a certain time—depends upon the transfer of an effective dose of the infectious agent from an infected individual to a susceptible one. After an epidemic has subsided, the affected host population contains relatively few susceptible individuals; thus reintroduction of the infection will not result in a new epidemic. Since the population of the infectious agent cannot reproduce itself in such a host population, the host population as a whole is immune to the epidemic disease, a circumstance termed herd immunity.

Following an epidemic, however, the host population gradually reverts to general susceptibility. This occurs largely because (1) the

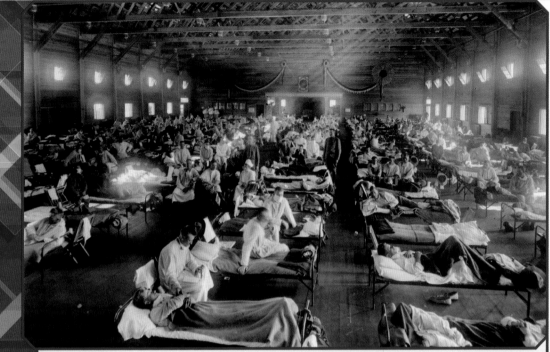

Temporary hospitals took in many influenza patients during the 1918–19 pandemic.

immunity of individuals deteriorates and (2) susceptible persons are added to the population by birth. In time the population as a whole again becomes susceptible. The time that elapses between successive epidemics is variable and differs from one disease to another.

The modern definition of epidemic has been expanded to include outbreaks of any chronic disease—as, for example, heart disease or cancer—influenced by the environment. The term "epidemic" is sometimes reserved for disease outbreaks among humans, whereas the term "epizootic" is used to describe epidemics among non-human animals.

In addition to providing clues to the causes of various diseases, epidemiologic studies are used to plan new health services, determine the incidence of various illnesses in a population, and to evaluate the overall health of a population. (In medicine, the term "incidence" refers to the number of new cases that occur during a certain period.) In most countries, public-health authorities regularly gather epidemiologic data on specific diseases and death rates in their populaces.

Descriptive Epidemiology

Epidemiologic studies may be classified as descriptive or analytic. In descriptive epidemiology, surveys are used to find out the nature of the population affected by a particular disease, noting such factors as age, sex, ethnic group, and occupation among those afflicted. Other descriptive studies may examine the occurrence of a disease over several years to determine changes or variations in incidence or death rates; geographic variations may also be noted. Descriptive studies also help to identify new disease syndromes or suggest previously unrecognized associations between risk factors and disease.

HISTORICAL EPIDEMICS

There have been many deadly epidemics throughout history. During the 1300s a pandemic of plague swept across the Eastern Hemisphere, ravaging populations in the Middle East, China, and Europe. Roughly 13 million people in China and 25 million people in Europe—perhaps as much as one-third of the population—died from the disease, which was called the Black Death. In 1918–19 a deadly influenza (flu) pandemic killed more than 20 million people worldwide.

Because of improvements in sanitation and in medicine, epidemics are not as common as they once were. There are, however, occasional outbreaks of diseases such as cholera and malaria in some parts of the world. The disease AIDS appeared in the 1980s and spread rapidly, especially in Africa. In 2003 a respiratory illness called SARS emerged in Asia and spread throughout the world within a few months. The H1N1 influenza pandemic of 2009, which began in Mexico, was the first major influenza outbreak in the 21st century.

To use the example of typhoid, a disease spread through contaminated food and water: when a large number of cases exhibiting certain symptoms is reported, it first becomes important to discover if the outbreak observed is truly caused by *Salmonella typhosa*, the typhoid organism. Once the diagnosis is established it is important to know the number of cases, whether the cases were scattered over the course of a year or occurred within a short period, and what the geographic distribution is. It is critically important that the precise addresses and activities of the patients be established. Two widely separated locations within a city might be found to have clusters of typhoid cases all arising at nearly the same time. It might be found that each of these clusters revolved about a family unit including cousins, nephews, and other friends, suggesting that in some way personal relationships might be important. Further investigation might show that all of the infected persons had dined at one time or at short intervals in a specific home. It might further be found that the person who had prepared the meal had recently visited a distant area and had suffered a mild attack of the disease, and was now spreading it to family and friends by unknowing contamination of food. This fictional case suggests the importance of studying the causes as well as the spread of disease.

Analytic Epidemiology

Analytic studies are carried out to test the conclusions made from descriptive surveys or laboratory observations. These studies divide a sample population into two or more groups

selected on the basis of a suspected cause of the disease—for example, cigarette smoking—and then monitor differences in incidence, death rates, or other variables.

Statistics are used to analyze the incidence of diseases and their prevalence. If, for example, a disease has an incidence rate of 100 cases per year in a given region, and, on the average, the affected persons live three years with the disease, the prevalence of the disease is 300. Statistical classification is another important tool in the study of possible causes of disease. For example, such studies, along with epidemiologic and nutritional analyses, have shown that diet is an important consideration in the causes of atherosclerosis (the buildup of fatty deposits on the walls of arteries). The statistical analyses drew attention to the role of high levels of animal fats and carbohydrates in the diet as possible causes of the disease. The analysis further drew attention to the fact that certain populations that do not eat much animal fat but instead live largely on vegetable oils and fish have a much lower incidence of atherosclerosis. Thus statistical surveys are of great importance in the study of human disease.

CHAPTER 5

SURGERY

Medicine treats disease with drugs, diet, irradiation, and other means. The treatment of injury and disease by manual or operative procedures is called surgery. The two fields are closely related. A physician practicing medicine must have a general knowledge of surgery, and the surgeon must be familiar, in general, with medical means of treatment, as well.

Surgery may be used for diagnosis—that is, to determine the cause of a disease. It may also be used to treat an injury or a disorder, to cure a disease, to relieve suffering, or to prolong life. Regardless of the reasons for surgery, the primary creed of the surgeon is: "If you cannot help, do not harm." Even if the surgery is unsuccessful, the surgeon is responsible for controlling the patient's pain before, during, and after surgery and for preventing or controlling infection that may result from opening the body during a surgical procedure.

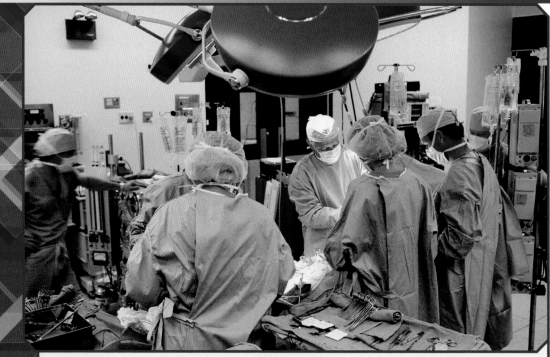

Surgeons, such as those shown here, use manual or operative procedures to treat injury and disease.

Over the years, as medical knowledge has increased and surgical procedures have grown more complex, areas of specialty have developed within the field of surgery. Surgeons who wish to practice in these fields must complete extensive training and must be certified by individual professional groups within the chosen specialty. Surgical specialists also exist in each of the medical fields that have developed as a result of medical specialization.

CATEGORIES OF SURGERY

There are five major categories of surgery—wound treatment, extirpative surgery, reconstructive surgery, physiological surgery, and transplantation—which are used in all surgical specialties. Surgeons must be thoroughly trained in each.

Wound treatment involves restoring injured tissues to normal by promoting healing and preventing infection. Because many surgical procedures themselves involve cutting through the skin and so inflicting a wound, wound treatment is part of almost any operation.

Extirpative surgery is the removal of diseased tissue or organs and includes all so-called radical operations. (Extirpation means the complete removal of a body part.) Reconstructive surgery is performed in order to restore injured or deformed body parts to normal. This category includes a wide range of complex operations, including reattachment of severed limbs and reconstruction or replacement of body parts.

Physiological surgery is a relatively new field wherein body functions are changed in order to eliminate or alleviate the symptoms of disease. One example is a surgical procedure in which the stomach of an overweight patient is made smaller. This procedure reduces the amount of food that the stomach can hold, so the patient can more easily control food intake. But it does not affect the underlying condition that originally caused the patient's weight problem. The fifth category, transplantation surgery, involves the grafting of tissue from one part of the body to another or the transfer of tissue from a donor to a recipient.

One category of surgery is transplantation, in which an organ, such as the kidney shown here, is transferred from a donor to a patient in need.

INSTRUMENTS AND TECHNIQUES

In some instances, the only instruments surgeons need are their hands. For example, surgeons may manipulate parts of the body to set simple bone fractures, to replace dislocated joints, or to move joints or vertebrae to relieve certain conditions. Often, however, the surgeon must enter the body to expose a disease.

To cut the skin, the surgeon uses a surgical knife, called a scalpel, with a sharp steel blade to make the cut as fine as possible. Some scalpels use a high-frequency electric arc to simultaneously cut and sterilize tissue. The surgeon may also use surgical scissors.

Hemostats control bleeding by clamping off blood vessels that have been severed in the progress of the operation. These vessels are then either tied off with fiber or cauterized—that is, sealed closed with a heated instrument. There are also clamps that will control blood flow without crushing delicate tissues. Sponges of absorbent cotton are used to absorb the blood that has leaked. These sponges are weighed to keep track of how much blood the patient loses during the operation. Forceps are used to hold back tissues so that the surgeons touch the tissues as little as possible.

COSMETIC SURGERY

Cosmetic surgery is surgery performed to improve a person's physical appearance (though in some cases the line between cosmetic and reconstructive surgery is blurred). Several different procedures can alter the contours of a person's features by adding, removing, or reshaping fat, skin, and other tissues. These procedures include rhinoplasty, to reconstruct the nose; otoplasty, to set back protruding ears; blepharoplasty, to remove excess fat and skin from the eyelids; abdominoplasty, to remove excess skin and fat in the abdomen; and rhytidectomy, or face-lift, to reduce facial wrinkles and sagging. In a face-lift, incisions are made in the scalp and behind the ears, and then the skin is pulled taut, trimmed, and sewn in place. In the procedure called liposuction, a tube is inserted through incisions in the skin and used to vacuum up deposits of fat just under the skin.

Cosmetic surgeons frequently also perform a variety of nonsurgical cosmetic procedures using lasers, injections, abrasion devices, and the application of chemicals. Common nonsurgical procedures include the removal of unwanted hair with a laser; chemical peels (chemical removal of the topmost layers of facial skin to minimize imperfections); and injections of botulinum toxin to temporarily paralyze muscles in the forehead and reduce wrinkles.

Retractors are used to open the wound and keep it open during the operation.

After an operation is finished, the tissues and skin are sewn together using a needle (usually curved) and fibers called sutures. Sutures are available in a variety of thicknesses and materials, and the surgeon selects those that will cause the least amount of injury to the tissues. Catgut sutures (made not from cat but from sheep intestines) can be left in the wound when it is closed because they will be absorbed by the body. Other sutures are made of silk, cotton, synthetic fiber, or even steel. These are not absorbed, but they may be used when extra strength is required.

Surgery also requires equipment for sterilizing surgical instruments and anything else that will touch or come close to the patient. Bacteria on instruments may be killed by using an autoclave—an apparatus that exposes the instruments to superheated steam under pressure—or by using chemicals. Surgeons and surgical staff wear sterile gowns, masks, and gloves to avoid contamination of the surgical site.

The surgical suite contains an abundance of equipment. Among the most basic are the machines used to administer anesthesia to the patient and to monitor the patient's vital signs—blood pressure, pulse rate, respiratory rate, and body temperature. A variety of highly sophisticated tools and techniques are also available to the modern surgeon. Stereotactic

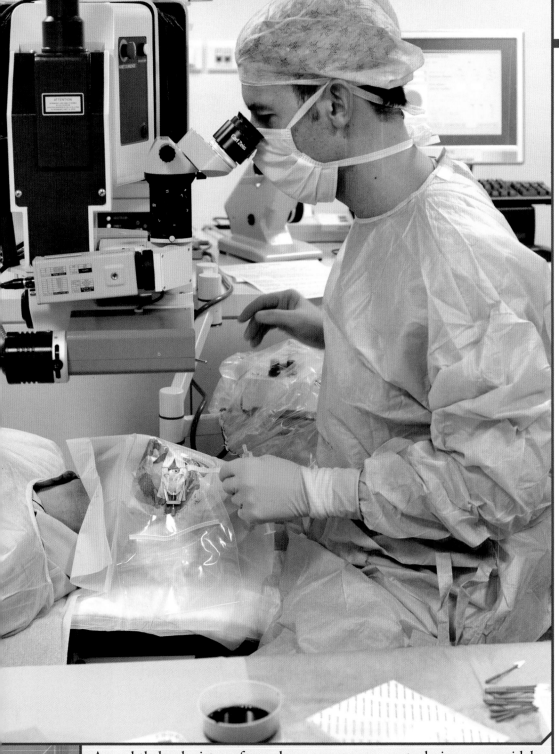

An ophthalmologist performs laser eye surgery—a technique now widely used to surgically reattach detached retinas and restore vision in patients with eye problems.

surgery, for example, uses X-ray photography to help brain surgeons guide the placement within the skull of electrodes, hollow tubes, or other objects. Lasers are now widely used to destroy tumors, some of which cannot be accessed by conventional surgery. Lasers are also used to surgically weld detached retinas back in place and to coagulate blood vessels to stop them from bleeding. The use of ultrasonics, or high-frequency sound waves, is valuable in neurosurgery and in the relief of inflamed muscle tissues. Ultrasonics have become an alternative to standard surgical operations for removing stones from the bladder, kidneys, and gallbladder. The sound waves break up the stones, which are then flushed from the body by natural processes.

CURRENT TRENDS IN SURGERY

During the late 20th and early 21st centuries, economic pressures and a better understanding of the body and its processes of healing brought about significant changes in the way surgery was conducted. Less invasive techniques, such as ultrasonics, were developed. Some traditional techniques of open surgery were replaced by the use of a thin, flexible

New technologies have allowed for more precise and advanced surgical techniques, including the use of robots to perform surgeries previously carried out directly by surgeons.

fiber-optic tube equipped with a light and a video connection; the tube, called an endoscope, could be inserted into various bodily passages to provide views of the interior of hollow organs or vessels. Accessories added to the endoscope allowed a variety of surgical procedures to be executed inside the body without making a major incision.

In many cases, radical operations have been replaced by more conservative procedures. In cases of breast cancer, for example, surgeons today are more likely to forgo radical mastectomy (removal of the entire breast and sometimes of additional tissue as well) in favor of lumpectomy, or removal of only the cancerous tumor.

Surgical operations are increasingly performed on an outpatient basis; relatively simple procedures that once required days of hospitalization are now completed in a few hours. More surgery is performed under local, rather than general, anesthesia, and patients are discharged earlier from the hospital to avoid the enfeebling effect of long bed rest.

The use of computers is growing, particularly in the development of sophisticated prostheses for disabled patients, in monitoring a severely ill patient, and as a means to aid the physician in making a diagnosis. In the field of tissue transplantation, researchers are developing better tissue-typing techniques, better ways of bypassing the immune system, and safer drugs to control rejection.

Surgeons also continue to look for alternatives to transplant surgery, and researchers are developing better biocompatible materials for artificial body parts. Other, more controversial areas of research include gene transplantation to correct genetic disorders, and operations on fetuses in utero (in the uterus).

CHAPTER 6

PHARMACOLOGY

P hysicians use special chemical compounds to diagnose, prevent, or treat certain kinds of diseases. These compounds are drugs. A more scientific name for them is pharmaceuticals. The science and art of preparing and standardizing drugs and dispensing them to the public is called pharmacy. Pharmacy encompasses many fields, including pharmacology—the broad science concerned with the sources of drugs, their physical and chemical properties, their actions in the body, and their use in the treatment of disease—and toxicology—the study of drugs' adverse, or toxic, effects. Those who practice pharmacy are pharmacists. Pharmacologists are scientists who study the properties and actions of drugs; toxicologists are scientists who study the toxicity of these agents.

As far back as history can be traced, including through Egyptian hieroglyphics, there are references to medicinal drugs recommended for various ailments. However, until the 20th century, only a few of the drugs mentioned or used really worked. Those that did work were based on "discovery"—accidental observations revealing that certain substances would ease pain or help cure an illness. In 1776, for example, English botanist and physician William Withering learned that an herbal tea made by an old farm woman was effective in treating dropsy, or excess water in the tissues, which is caused by the inability of the heart to pump strongly enough. He found that one ingredient of the tea, which was made with leaves of the foxglove plant (*Digitalis purpurea*), strengthened the heart's pumping ability. The drug made from the foxglove is now known as digitalis and is a standard treatment for many heart ailments.

While finding drugs through discovery did yield a few important vaccines

Foxglove (*Digitalis purpurea*) has been found to be effective as a treatment for many heart ailments.

and medicines, it was not until the 20th century that the new method of inventing drugs based on science made it possible to treat, cure, or prevent a host of diseases. To invent a useful drug it was first necessary to understand far more about how the body worked, why disease occurred, and why and how certain chemicals acted in the body. These tasks comprise the focus of the science of pharmacology.

WHERE DRUGS COME FROM

Drugs are obtained from many different sources. Some come from plants, while others come from animals or minerals. Since plant and animal tissues are not the same from one organism to another, one of the first problems pharmacologists had to solve was that of uniform dosage. For example, belladonna, a drug that is sometimes used to treat stomach cramps, comes from a plant called nightshade. All nightshade plants, however, do not contain the same amount of belladonna. Physicians could not know whether the doses of belladonna that they prescribed were too strong or too weak. To solve this problem, researchers assumed that only a certain part of the crude drug had the ability to act on the body. This

Today most drugs are produced synthetically in chemical laboratories, yielding more effective and safer drugs than in the past.

they called the active principle, and they set themselves the task of finding and standardizing this component.

Eventually the active principles of various crude drugs were isolated. The active principles could be measured, allowing precise quantities to be put into powders, tablets, capsules, and other medicinal vehicles. Drugs in these forms could either be prescribed by a physician or bought freely over the counter. The doctor now knew exactly how much of a given drug he or she was prescribing and could tell within reason what effects the prescription would have on a patient.

Today most drugs are no longer derived by isolating and purifying crude plants or tissues. Instead they are synthesized, or made, in chemical laboratories. For example, when the drug cortisone was discovered, it was produced at great cost from the adrenal glands of dead animals. Later, scientists learned how to make the drug from the bile of slaughtered oxen at a lower cost. Still later it was synthesized from a variety of easily available plants. The synthetic drugs that duplicate the active principles of plants, animals, or minerals are superior to natural substances because they contain only the active principles, with impurities and other useless substances eliminated.

BIOLOGICALS

Some substances derived from animal sources and used as drugs are not obtained from dead animals. Biologicals are such substances. They are made from infectious organisms taken from the body of a live animal or even a human. Tetanus toxoid, which is used to immunize persons against tetanus, or lockjaw, is such a biological. It is made in this way: a small quantity of *Clostridium tetani* (the bacteria that cause tetanus) is injected into a broth-like liquid in a large tank called a

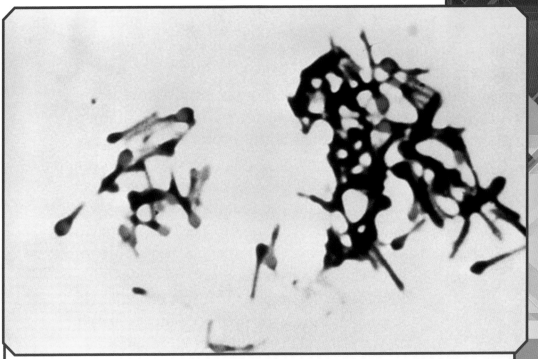

Clostridium tetani, the causative agent of tetanus, is used to produce tetanus toxoid, a biological.

fermenter. Within this nutritious liquid, the bacteria grow and reproduce and also produce tetanus toxin. After a while the bacteria are removed from the broth and destroyed. The remaining tetanus toxin is removed from the broth and then chemically treated to render it harmless. However, this "poisonless" toxin, or toxoid, retains the power to stimulate in a person's blood the formation of antibodies against tetanus toxin. Thus the manufactured toxoid can be injected into children, frequently along with other vaccines against diphtheria and pertussis, to immunize them against tetanus infection.

SYNTHETICS

A number of synthetic drugs are not duplicates of natural substances. Just as the invention of drugs was an enormous advance over the time when drugs could be found only through accidental discovery, science now is capable of designing entirely new drugs not found in nature.

One way by which new drugs are designed is by modifying the molecular structure of other drugs. Such modified drugs, called analogues, are often more effective, cause fewer side effects, and can be produced more cheaply than the original drug. Thus, to eliminate some of the serious side effects of cortisone, and to increase its potency, scientists modified its molecular structure to get prednisone, hydrocortisone, and a number of other analogues.

While this kind of molecular manipulation is an important source of new drugs, there is yet another way to make new medicines—genetic engineering. This technique involves altering the genetic code of bacteria, thereby turning them into tiny drug-manufacturing factories. This method can make bacteria produce substances they would not normally make, such as human growth hormone or insulin.

Researchers are constantly developing and testing new synthetic drugs to create safer, more effective treatments against disease.

How Drugs Act

Drugs act by changing the way some of the cells in the body behave. Although people speak often of the effect of a drug, what one actually sees is a change in the way the body is working. For example, aspirin does not by itself reduce fever. Rather, it temporarily affects the nerve cells in the brain that regulate body temperature. Changing—that is,

Drug Standards and Regulation

The United States Pharmacopeia (USP) was founded in 1820 as a nongovernmental authority to establish criteria for the strength and purity of commonly used medicinal products. It evolved into the official standards-setting authority for all prescription (ethical) drugs and nonprescription (proprietary) drugs, as well as other health care products manufactured or sold in the country. More than 130 other countries rely on USP standards, and a product's meeting those standards is globally viewed as assurance of high quality. The USP publishes its standards for drugs in two compendia—the *United States Pharmacopeia* and the *National Formulary*. The former provides detailed information on all active drug substances, while the latter covers inactive ingredients.

The Food and Drug Administration (FDA), an agency within the U.S. Department of Health and Human Services, is responsible for assuring the safety, effectiveness, and security of human drugs taken by millions of Americans. (The agency also oversees veterinary drugs, biological products, medical devices, the country's food supply, cosmetics, and products that emit radiation.) The FDA rigorously evaluates all new prescription and over-the-counter (OTC) drugs before they are approved for marketing and serves as a consumer watchdog for the more than 10,000 drugs on the market.

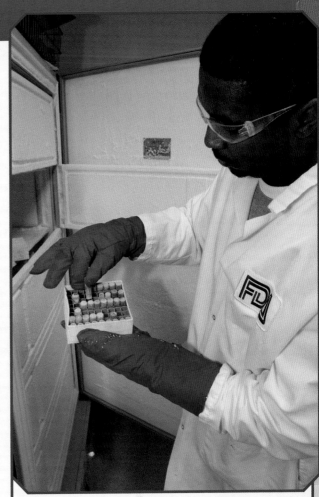

An FDA microbiologist freezes evidence for a later court date. The FDA oversees the safety and effectiveness of drugs developed and prescribed in the United States.

stimulating or depressing—the normal way a cell or tissue acts is one of the two main ways by which drugs act in the body. Drugs that act in this way are called pharmacodynamic agents. The other way by which drugs act involves destroying or slowing the growth of disease-causing organisms without affecting the body's normal cells. Drugs that act in this way are called chemotherapeutic agents. Antibiotics such as penicillin, streptomycin, tetracycline, and the sulfa drugs are chemotherapeutic agents. Anticancer drugs, which work by destroying or slowing the growth of cancer cells, also are categorized as chemotherapeutic agents.

REACTIONS TO DRUGS

In order for a chemical to be considered a drug it must have the capacity to affect how the body works—to be biologically active. No substance that has the power to do this is completely safe, and drugs are approved only after they demonstrate that they are relatively safe when used as directed and when the benefits outweigh their risks. Thus, some very dangerous drugs are approved because they are necessary to treat serious illness. Digitalis, which causes the heart muscle to contract, is a dangerous drug, but doctors are permitted to use it because it is vital for treating patients whose heart muscle is weak. A drug as potent as digitalis would not be approved to treat such minor ailments as temporary fatigue because the risks outweigh the benefits.

Many persons suffer ill effects from drugs even though they take the drug exactly as directed by the doctor or the label. The human population, unlike a colony of ants or bees, contains a great variety of genetic variation. Drugs are tested on at most a few thousand people. When that same drug is taken by millions, some people may not respond in a predictable way to the drug. This is called having an idiosyncratic response. An example of this would be a person who responds to a particular sedative by become excited rather than relaxed. Other examples include being hypersensitive, or extremely sensitive, to certain drugs, suffering reactions that resemble allergies.

A patient may also acquire a tolerance for a certain drug. This means that ever-larger doses are necessary to produce the desired therapeutic effect. Tolerance may lead to habituation, in which the person becomes so dependent upon the drug that he or she becomes addicted to it. Addiction causes severe psychological and physical disturbances when the drug is taken

The use of thalidomide as a sedative by pregnant women in the 1950s and 1960s led to an increase in children born with phocomelia, a congenital deformity.

away. Morphine, cocaine, and amphetamines are common habit-forming drugs.

Finally, drugs often have unwanted side effects. These usually cause only minor discomfort such as a skin rash, headache, or drowsiness. Certain drugs, however, can produce serious, even life-threatening adverse reactions. For example, the drug thalidomide was once called one of the safest sedatives ever developed. However, in the late 1950s and early 1960s thousands of women in the United Kingdom who took it during pregnancy to treat nausea gave birth to seriously deformed babies, and the drug was taken off the market. (Later, however, thalidomide was found to be effective in treating cachexia, the severe weight loss that occurs in patients with diseases such as AIDS, tuberculosis, and leprosy, and the drug was reintroduced for use in this patient population.)

Adverse reactions also can stem from mixing drugs. For example, taking aspirin, which has blood-thinning qualities, for a headache can be very harmful if one is also taking other blood-thinning drugs such as heparin or dicumarol.

CONCLUSION

In 2014 the U.S. FDA approved 41 novel drugs, the most new agents approved by the organization in a single year over the last decade. The newly approved drugs included some of the first agents available for the treatment of chronic hepatitis C and metastatic melanoma (a form of skin cancer that has spread to tissues throughout the body). Agents also were approved to treat some rare diseases, such as leishmaniasis and Gaucher disease, for which few or no treatments previously had been available. Scientists also continued to make progress in the development of bioengineered tissues, which can be used to replace diseased or damaged tissues. In 2015 researchers applied techniques from tissue engineering to create a semi-functioning bioartificial rat limb, representing a significant step forward for regenerative medicine and artificial-limb research. Such groundbreaking progress is critical to the advance of modern medicine, where novel therapies capable of saving lives and improving quality of life are greatly desired.

angioplasty Surgical repair of a blocked blood vessel, usually via passage of a balloon catheter through the vessel to the area of blockage.

auscultation The act of listening to sounds arising within organs (as the lungs) as an aid to diagnosis and treatment.

bloodletting The removal of blood from a patient to treat illness or disease.

cardiovascular Of, relating to, or involving the heart and blood vessels.

cauterize To burn with a hot iron or a chemical substance to destroy infected tissue or to close a wound during surgery.

chorea Any of various nervous disorders (of humans or dogs) marked by irregular and involuntary movements of muscle groups in various parts of the body.

congenital Existing at or dating from birth.

diagnostician A person who makes diagnoses.

emetic A medicine or other substance that causes vomiting.

erysipelas An acute contagious infection of the skin and underlying tissue, characterized by fever and intense inflammation, and caused by a hemolytic streptococcus bacteria.

hemodialysis The process of removing blood from an individual (as of a patient with failing kidneys), purifying it by dialysis, and then returning it to the person's bloodstream.

homeostasis The ability of the body to maintain a stable internal environment despite changes in external conditions.

inoculate To introduce material (as a vaccine) into the body, especially by injection to protect against or treat a disease.

lymphocyte Any of the white blood cells that arise in the bone marrow that are found especially in lymphoid tissue (as of the lymph nodes and spleen), blood, and lymph, and play a key role in the immune response.

macrophage A large cell of the immune system that takes in and breaks down foreign material and waste.

nephron A single unit of the kidney that functions in filtering the blood and forming urine from waste products.

ophthalmoscope An optical instrument for viewing the inside of the eye.

pandemic An outbreak of disease occurring over a wide area and affecting many people.

paralysis Complete or partial loss of function especially when involving motion or sensation in a part of the body.

phocomelia A congenital deformity in which the limbs are extremely shortened so that the feet and hands arise close to the trunk.

practitioner A person who works in a professional medical or legal business.

quarantine To isolate a person with a contagious disease for a period of time.

sanitation The promotion of community hygiene and disease prevention especially by maintaining sewage systems, by collecting and disposing of trash and garbage, and by cleaning streets.

secretion A substance produced and released by a gland.

shunt A device (as a narrow tube) used to establish a surgical passage to divert a bodily fluid (as blood) from one vessel or part to another.

slit lamp A lamp for projecting a narrow beam of intense light that is used in conjunction with a biomicroscope for examining the anterior parts (as the conjunctiva or cornea) of an eye.

strabismus Inability of one eye to attain binocular vision with the other because of imbalance of the muscles of the eyeball.

trepan To use a surgical instrument known as a trephine to cut out and remove circular sections of the skull.

virulence The relative capacity of a pathogen to overcome body defenses.

vivisection Operating or experimenting on a living animal for scientific or medical study.

Canadian Medical Hall of Fame
267 Dundas Street, Suite 202
London, ON N6A 1H2
Canada
(519) 488-2003
Website: http://cdnmedhall.org
Established in 1994, the Canadian Medical
Hall of Fame honors important Canadian
physicians and public health figures
whose work has advanced medical science in that country. The organization
works to advance and improve the
quality of health care through educational opportunities and cooperation
with a network of affiliated medical
associations.

Indiana Medical History Museum (IMHM)
3045 West Vermont Street
Indianapolis, IN 46222
(317) 635-7329
Website: http://www.imhm.org
Housed in the facilities of the former
Central State Hospital (whose former
pathology building is on the United
States Register of Historic Places), the

IMHM has an amphitheater, laboratories, a library, an autopsy room, and an anatomical museum—all of which serve to educate the public on medical science and the history of medicine.

International Museum of Surgical Science (IMSS)
1524 North Lake Shore Drive
Chicago, IL 60610
(312) 642-6502
Website: https://www.imss.org
A division of the International College of Surgeons, the IMSS holds a permanent collection of medical artifacts, rare manuscripts, and artwork related to the history of medicine as well as exhibits on developments in surgery and medical technology. It also facilitates on-site educational programs and provides classroom materials to educators.

Museum of Health Care
Ann Baillie Building National Historic Site
32 George Street
Kingston, ON K7L 2V7
Canada
(613) 548-2419
Website: http://www.museumofhealthcare.ca

The Museum of Health Care has on-site and digital exhibits dedicated to the history of health care in Canada, including exhibits on vaccines and immunization, pharmacology, and the administration of health care during wars and other conflicts.

National Museum of Health and Medicine (NMHM)
2500 Linden Lane
Silver Spring, MD 20910
(301) 319-3300
Website: http://www.medicalmuseum.mil
Established as the Army Medical Museum during the American Civil War, the NMHM has been a key organization in the study of anatomy and pathology for over 150 years. In addition to its library and archives, the museum has been involved in successful campaigns to promote immunization, sexual health, and pathological research.

World Health Organization (WHO)
Avenue Appia 20
1211 Geneva 27
Switzerland
Website: http://www.who.int/en/

WHO is the premier organization working internationally to promote public health, channel funds and medical training into regions in need, and eradicate the spread of disease globally.

WEBSITES

Because of the changing nature of Internet links, Rosen Publishing has developed an online list of websites related to the subject of this book. This site is updated regularly. Please use this link to access this list:

http://www.rosenlinks.com/SCI/Med

FOR FURTHER READING

Aldridge, Susan. *Trailblazers in Medicine*. New York, NY: Rosen Publishing, 2015.

Allman, Toney. *Medieval Medicine and Disease* (The Library of Medieval Times). San Diego, CA: ReferencePoint Press, 2015.

Barber, Nicola. *Medieval Medicine* (Medicine through the Ages). Chicago, IL: Raintree, 2013.

Davies, Gill. *The Illustrated Timeline of Medicine*. New York, NY: Rosen Publishing, 2012.

Hand, Carol. *Epidemiology: The Fight Against Ebola & Other Diseases*. Minneapolis, MN: ABDO Publishing, 2015.

Hand, Carol. *Vaccines* (Medical Marvels). Minneapolis, MN: ABDO Publishing, 2014.

Hardman, Lizabeth. *The History of Medicine*. Detroit, MI: Lucent Books, 2012.

Hollar, Sherman, ed. *Pioneers in Medicine: From the Classical World to Today*. New York, NY: Britannica Educational Publishing, 2013.

Langley, Andrew. *Ancient Medicine* (Medicine Through the Ages). Chicago, IL: Raintree, 2012.

Lew, Kristi. *Advances in Medicine*. New York, NY: Cavendish Square, 2014.

Oxlade, Chris. *Modern Medicine* (Medicine Through the Ages). Chicago, IL: Raintree, 2012.

Rooney, Anne. *The History of Medicine* (The History of Science). New York, NY: Rosen Publishing, 2013.

Spilsbury, Richard. *The Pharmaceutical Industry*. London, UK: Wayland, 2014.

Zott, Lynn M. *Alternative Medicine* (Opposing Viewpoints). Detroit, MI: Greenhaven Press, 2012.